L.C. 1/10/68

D0934207

Biddle's Bank

Biddle's Bank

THE CRUCIAL YEARS

JEAN ALEXANDER WILBURN

Columbia University Press

NEW YORK & LONDON 1967

EDWARD MINER GALLAUDET MEMORIAL LIBRARY
GALLAUDET COLLEGE
WASHINGTON, D. C.

*Jean Alexander Wilburn is Assistant Professor
of Economics at Barnard College*

COPYRIGHT © 1964, 1967 COLUMBIA UNIVERSITY PRESS

First published in book form 1967

LIBRARY OF CONGRESS CATALOG CARD NUMBER: 67-12536

PRINTED IN THE UNITED STATES OF AMERICA

332.1
W66b

Acknowledgments

THE WAR against the Second Bank of the United States has been written of frequently and knowledgeably. It would, therefore, never have occurred to me to attempt research in this field had not Professor Carter Goodrich recognized an important aspect of the subject, the support of the Bank, which remained somewhat unclear. I must thank him not only for suggesting the topic but also for devoting many hours to interested criticism.

I am greatly indebted to Professor Eric McKitrick of Columbia University for the genuine enthusiasm he showed for what I was attempting and for his early recognition and recommendation of the primary source material which would provide the background for any fresh perspective of the Second Bank.

It was most generous of Professors Joseph Dorfman and Stuart Bruchey to read the manuscript and offer many valuable suggestions as to how it might be improved. I, of course, bear final responsibility for any interpretations attempted.

JEAN ALEXANDER WILBURN

Columbia University
July, 1966

99928

Contents

Maps

Tables

Biddle's Bank

I

Introduction

TWENTIETH CENTURY historians of the Second United States Bank excel in imaginative scholarship and persuasive rhetoric. Can any student of American economic history fail to be impressed by the thoroughness and thoughtful devotion Bray Hammond has given to the subject in his *Banks and Politics in America?* Or is it possible to react passively to the dynamic and quick arguments of a Schlesinger? More recently, Marvin Meyers in *The Jacksonian Persuasion* has written with impressive insight and originality. Taking into account earlier writers on the subject such as Beard and Catterall, we would think enough had been written for us to have a very clear idea of the Bank's friends and enemies. On the contrary, very little has been said about the other side—about the support which the Bank had. A reading of the literature leaves the impression that its only support consisted of a few thousand stockholders, the Bank's employees, and a handful of statesmen.

For historians of the Bank, the emphasis has been upon explaining its defeat and upon identifying those people, or the convictions they held, that were responsible for its downfall. Bray Hammond, describing the forces acting against the Bank, wrote: "The Jacksonians were unconventional and skillful in politics. In their assault on the Bank they united five important elements, which, incongruities notwithstanding, comprised an effective combination. These were Wall Street's jealousy of Chestnut Street, the business man's dislike of the federal Bank's restraint upon bank credit, the politician's resentment at the Bank's interference with states' rights, popular identification of the Bank with the aristocracy of business, and the direction of agrarian antipathy away from banks in general to the federal Bank in particular." [1] Schlesinger analyzed the situation somewhat differently: "The war against the Bank thus enlisted the enthusiastic support of two basically antagonistic groups: on the one hand, debtor interests of the West and local banking interests of the East; on the other, eastern workingmen and champions of the radical Jeffersonian tradition." [2] If we add Catterall's [3] list of opponents to those of Hammond and Schlesinger, we find these writers have already claimed as enemies of the Bank the strict constructionists, states' righters, state bankers, the poor, western debtors, eastern workingmen, Wall Street speculators, the business man, agrarians, champions of the radical Jeffersonian tradition, and people devoted to the principle of equality or democracy. So broad a spectrum of opposition to the Bank is offered, that we are naturally led to question how the "Bank War" could have continued for so long and been waged as fiercely as it has been described, if the two groups were so unevenly matched.

Could the quality of the support have been so superior as to counterbalance the formidable array of its enemies? We read just the opposite. High caliber statesmen such as Calhoun and Clay, though favoring the Bank, are represented as not effectively supporting it because of being distracted by the questions of nullification and personal ambitions for the Presidency. Even a lesser statesman such as George McDuffie of South Carolina, always in favor of the Bank, was criticized for giving precedence to the tariff issue at a critical period for the Bank. [4] The other group described as supporters, the stockholders and employees, appears by 1829 to have been rather passive, content to let Nicholas Biddle do as he wished.

[1] Bray Hammond, *Banks and Politics in America* (Princeton: Princeton University Press, 1957), p. 329.

[2] Arthur M. Schlesinger, Jr., *The Age of Jackson* (Boston: Little, Brown & Co., 1950), p. 79.

[3] Ralph C. H. Catterall, *The Second Bank of the United States* (Chicago: University of Chicago Press, 1903), p. 164.

[4] *Ibid.*, p. 229. Footnote 9 gives John Quincy Adams' and Ingersoll's criticisms of McDuffie.

As Walter B. Smith recognized, the Second Bank has been a favorite topic for historians because of its involvement in politics.[5] Consequently, interpretations of the Jacksonian Era and its relation to the Bank have tended to be more political than economic. This has not been just a matter of the personal interest of the authors, but also was characteristic of their source material. Although bibliographies in this field are very extensive and show considerable variety, there is a core of books from which most information is drawn and which is quoted most frequently. The authors were either politicians of the Jacksonian Era, such as Thomas Benton, James Hamilton, William Seward, and Thurlow Weed, or else they were biographers of such leading politicians as Daniel Webster, Henry Clay, and the members of Andrew Jackson's cabinet. Even the most frequently used letters from the Biddle Manuscripts are letters between Biddle and the leading politicians. The emphasis on the political atmosphere in the source material is so heavy that other aspects—which could be important in evaluating the Bank War—are obscured. To Schlesinger, Hammond, and their predecessors, certain groups were Jacksonian and therefore destroyed the Bank. But in the later publications of Meyers and Lee Benson, what was formerly the cause now became the effect—the Bank War forged and gave the character to the Jacksonian Party.[6] No additional writing is needed to close the circle.

In an effort, then, to hold the personal and political bias of the early material to a minimum, a somewhat more objective approach will be attempted in this study.

Since there was no act more final or decisive in the life of the United States Bank than a congressman's vote in the national legislature on the question of whether the Bank would or would not be rechartered, we shall begin looking for support by exam-

[5] Walter B. Smith, *Economic Aspects of the Second Bank of the United States* (Cambridge: Harvard University Press, 1953), p. 1.
[6] Marvin Meyers, *The Jacksonian Persuasion; Politics and Belief* (Stanford: Stanford University Press, 1957), p. 57.

ining the geographical distribution of votes cast in the United States Congress on certain crucial questions pertaining to the Bank. The results are of sufficient interest to warrant the application of the same technique to the New York State legislature to see whether the national trend is reflected in that state.

After the analysis of national and state voting patterns, we shall focus attention on an examination of memorials sent to Congress by state banks, state legislatures, and groups of citizens. It was the accepted custom during this period for constituents to make their attitudes on current questions, such as the tariff, public lands, and internal improvements, known to Congress through the use of memorials or petitions to the Senate and House of Representatives. On the one hand, these memorials could embody long detailed explanations as to why those affixing their signatures felt as they did about a public issue, or, at the opposite extreme, they could be simple requests for Congress to vote in favor or against a particular measure. Whatever their form, however, they represent tangible evidence of support or hostility towards the subject of their contents, in this case toward the Second United States Bank. As such, they will be used to locate support of the Bank, quantitatively when the material permits, to analyze their geographic distribution, and to evaluate the economic significance of their contents for certain crucial areas.

2

Congressional Support

IT WILL BE recalled that the charter of the Second United States Bank was to expire in 1836. Hence the question of whether to recharter it need not have arisen as early as 1832. Clay, Webster, and many others, including the Bank's own lobbyists in Washington, advised Biddle to proceed at once with a request for a renewal of the charter of the Bank. Biddle concurred and the bill for recharter was presented to Congress in January of 1832.

Opinions differ as to why Biddle finally decided, after considerable deliberation, to introduce a memorial requesting the Bank's recharter as early as January, 1832. According to Thomas Payne Govan, whose statements are well documented, Biddle, Henry Clay, and most informed political observers believed Jackson was sure to win reelection in the fall of 1832, and the decision to apply for recharter was based solely on what was thought to be the wisest policy for the Bank. There was a faint hope that Jackson might sign the new charter if presented to him prior to the election, but the conviction was held that he would not do so if he won reelection without having accepted or rejected the renewal. By raising the issue before the campaign, Biddle thought the candidates for Congress would be forced to express themselves with respect to the recharter if Jackson vetoed the bill. It was believed that the people wanted both Jackson and the Bank. The possibility existed, then, that two-thirds of the congressmen to be elected in November of 1832 would be forced to commit themselves to vote for the recharter.[1]

[1] Thomas Payne Govan, *Nicholas Biddle, Nationalist and Public Banker, 1786–1844* (Chicago: University of Chicago Press, 1959), p. 172.

It was not only the pro-Bank men but also the Bank's enemies who believed it stood in high popular favor.[2] The vote in both Senate and House on whether to recharter the Bank supported their position. The bill passed the Senate 28–20 [3] and the House by 107–85.[4] Jackson then vetoed it in July, 1832. The bill was returned to the Senate immediately, but a two-thirds majority could not be mustered to override the veto. The Bank was then made a campaign issue, and Clay was resoundingly defeated.

Prior to Jackson's veto in July of 1832 the Bank was not caught up in politics as extensively as afterward. At the Baltimore convention of May, 1832, at which Van Buren was nominated for vice-president and Jackson chosen unanimously to succeed himself, there was no agreement on an Address to the electorate. The state delegations were advised to "make such a report or address to their constituents as they might think proper." [5] The New York Address, published three weeks before Jackson vetoed the bill for recharter, made states' rights the major issue between the parties. The Bank issue was not treated prominently.

The vote of 1832 on whether to recharter the Bank will be the first vote presented, since it had the advantage of being cast before the Veto and therefore before the Bank became a major political issue. (See Map 1, and Table 1, pp. 8–9).

It is surprising in view of commonly held beliefs to find that the West favored the Bank. Equally surprising are the diametrically opposed positions in New England. Vermont, Massachusetts, Connecticut, and Rhode Island were all 100 per cent in

[2] Hezekiah Niles, *The Weekly Register* (Baltimore, 1813–1841), January 9, 1832. Representative Wayne is quoted as stating in the House that the subject of the Bank had been brought before the House at that time to bring odium on those who should oppose it.

[3] *Abridgement of the Debates of Congress*, vol. XI, p. 753.

[4] *Register of Debates in Congress*, vol. VIII, p. 1074.

[5] Lee Benson, *The Concept of Jacksonian Democracy; New York as a Test Case* (Princeton: Princeton University Press, 1961), p. 51, quoted from the *Albany Argus*, June 26, 1832, pp. 1–2.

favor of the Bank, yet New Hampshire and Maine stood almost as forcefully against it by 86 and 67 per cent respectively. New York, anti-Bank, but adjacent to vigorously pro-Bank middle states, is significant especially when the large number of votes of that state is considered. That the South was heavily anti-Bank runs true to most interpretations, but the complete support of Louisiana has never been singled out for comment. This gains in importance when it is seen that two years later Louisiana would again support the Bank with a 100 per cent vote in its favor.

It might be rewarding to look at another interpretation of the vote of 1832.

In 1902 Ralph Catterall wrote what is considered the basic history of the Second United States Bank. It is included in most bibliographies of subsequent writers on the Bank and is authoritatively quoted by them. After mentioning the size of both the House and Senate vote, Catterall proceeded to analyze only the Senate vote. He wrote:

The vote in the Senate is significant of the position of various parts of the Union on the question. All the New England senators voted aye excepting Hill of New Hampshire; of the senators from the middle states only three were opposed, those from New York and one from New Jersey. In the South and Southwest only three were favorable, those from Louisiana and one from Mississippi. All the Western states were favorable excepting Kentucky, Illinois, and Missouri, which divided their votes. *The determined opposition was from the South and Southwest* (italics mine).[6]

When Catterall said, "All the New England senators voted aye excepting Hill of New Hampshire," the meaning of this statement for all intents and purposes is that New England was 100 per cent pro-Bank. Isaac Hill's opposition should be regarded not as representative of the section of the country so much as a quirk attributable to his own personality. He is de-

[6] Ralph C. H. Catterall, *The Second Bank of the United States* (Chicago: University of Chicago Press, 1903), p. 235.

MAP I

United States House and Senate Vote, *1832*

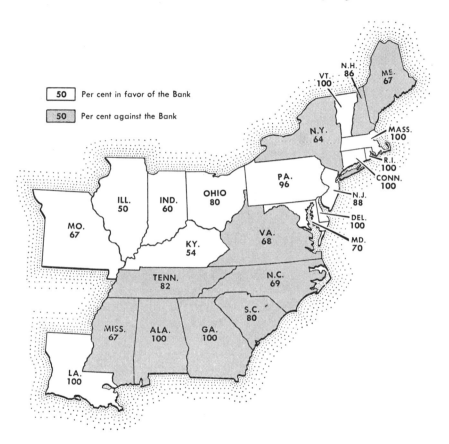

TABLE I

United States House and Senate Vote, 1832

	House		Senate	
	For	Against	For	Against
Maine	1	6	2	0
New Hampshire	0	5	1	1
Vermont	3	0	2	0
Connecticut	6	0	2	0
Massachusetts	12	0	2	0
Rhode Island	2	0	2	0
New York	12	19	0	2
New Jersey	6	0	1	1
Pennsylvania	24	1	2	0
Delaware	1	0	2	0
Maryland	5	3	2	0
Kentucky	6	5	1	1
Mississippi	0	1	1	1
Alabama	0	3	0	2
Georgia	0	6	0	2
Virginia	6	11	0	2
North Carolina	4	7	0	2
South Carolina	2	6	0	2
Tennessee	2	7	0	2
Louisiana	3	0	2	0
Ohio	10	3	2	0
Illinois			1	1
Indiana	1	2	2	0
Missouri	1	0	1	1

scribed thus: "He was frail and lame, an abusive editorial writer, an acrid partisan, ..." [7] "He had the rancorous malignity of those men who have been in a contest with persons who have treated them from above downwards." [8]

The rhetorical implication of Catterall's statement about the middle states is that they were pro-Bank. There is no highlighting of the decisive role New York played. Nor has he drawn the sharp contrast between Louisiana and the adjacent territory Everything is oriented towards his generalization: "The determined opposition was from the South and Southwest."

Through failure to analyze the House vote the problem is oversimplified and a generalization easily come by. Only when the vote of each house is considered are we alerted to the strength of the New York opposition, the split in New England, and Louisiana's singular role. Examination of these areas might have led subsequent writers to significantly different interpretations. One of the most recent writers on the Jacksonian era, G. G. Van Deusen, said, "Really formidable opposition came only from the West and Southwest." [9] To support his statement Van Deusen gave as reference Catterall's analysis of the senatorial vote. It should be noted that Catterall's regions, *South* and Southwest, here became *West* and Southwest.

Another aspect of Catterall's analysis has led to confusion: Exactly which states he included in the Southwest is not clear. He must have included more than just Mississippi and Louisiana since three of four senators voted pro-Bank in these states. Tennessee must have been considered as belonging to the Southwest because Catterall did not include it among the western states.

[7] Bray Hammond, *Banks and Politics in America* (Princeton: Princeton University Press, 1957), p. 331.

[8] *Ibid.*, as quoted from William G. Sumner, *Andrew Jackson* (Boston, 1882), p. 186.

[9] G. G. Van Deusen, *The Jacksonian Era* (New York: Harper Bros., 1959), p. 65.

Mississippi, Louisiana, and Tennessee taken together as the Southwest showed three votes against the Bank and three votes pro-Bank. Hence he must have included in the Southwest Alabama and perhaps Georgia along with Mississippi, Louisiana, and Tennessee. The "determined opposition" came, then, from Tennessee and from states which today are included in the South, viz., Virginia, North and South Carolina, Georgia, and Alabama. It is doubtful that Tennessee, Jackson's home state, should be given a "regional" interpretation. Hence the regional opposition to which Catterall referred would today be called "southern opposition."

That he referred to it as the "South and Southwest" is unfortunate on two counts. First, it kept him from drawing the generalization that except for Jackson's home state, the Southwest and West gave strong support to the Bank. Had he viewed the Southwest as Tennessee, Mississippi, and Louisiana, this is the conclusion to which he must have come. Second, as was pointed out earlier, his conclusion that the *South* and Southwest presented the determined opposition has developed into the belief that the *West* and Southwest presented the really formidable opposition—just the contrary to the true state of affairs.

There is one final distortion in Catterall's analysis which resulted from the peculiar nature of what is reflected by the senatorial vote.

It is surprising that about one half of the senators who voted against the Bank were actually men who were known to be, or had expressed themselves to have been, in favor of the Bank.[10] Indeed, some had actively fought for the Bank. How was it, then, that they voted against the institution? Very simply, these men felt it more important to support Jackson *at this time*, just prior to the election, than to hurt his chances of reelection by

---

[10] Letter of Thomas Cadwalader to Nicholas Biddle, November 12, 1831, The Papers of Nicholas Biddle (Manuscripts Division, Library of Congress, Washington, D.C.). Cited hereafter as NBP.

placing him in the position of having to veto or sign a bill on the Bank. If the bill for recharter failed in Congress, no comment from Jackson would be required. They really wanted the whole issue of the renewal to be brought up in the following session of Congress after the election in the fall was over. But failing this, the least they could do was to keep it from passing Congress then.

There are many letters in the Biddle Manuscripts to support this point of view, and the following is typical:

Thomas Cadwalader to Biddle [11]

Barnard's—Wash.
21.Dec.1831

(Private)
My dear Sir,

I yesterday reported my arrival. I have had this morning a long and frank conversation with Mr. McLane.[12] He says *positively* [13] that the President will reject the Bill, *if the matter is agitated this* Session. He (the President) and those about him would regard the movement, before the election, as an act of hostility, or as founded on the idea that his opinions would bend to personal views, and that his fears would induce him to truckle. Mr. McLane is sure that under such circumstances he would apply his veto, even if certain that he would thereby lose the Election. The question he says cannot now be started without being regarded as a party one, and the influence of the government would be thrown upon *it* so that we should lose a large number of votes which under other circumstances we should gain—the rejection not being considered as a final one—as the question may be renewed at the next session, or a subsequent one, the Veto once given the President would never swerve, and that two-thirds would be required on any subsequent trial. Accordingly to the Secretary's view of it, therefore, we are now to see whether we can rely on two-thirds under the circumstances averted to, namely the operation of party feeling, and Government influence and to

[11] *Correspondence of Nicholas Biddle*, ed. by Reginald C. McGrane (Boston: Houghton Mifflin Co., 1919), pp. 147–48.
[12] Secretary of the Treasury under Jackson.
[13] All italicized passages in this letter are italicized in the original.

that inquiry I devote myself. Mr. McLane seems to have canvassed
the Senate thoroughly, and we have gone over the names together.
He gives us—Maine, Massachusetts, Rhode Island, Connecticut and
Vermont—two each
and New Hampshire making   11
New Jersey 2.—but if this session, strike off Dicker-
    son—say then   1
.   .   .   .   . Maryland (if *this Session*, we lose
                     Smith!!! for *certain*),   1
N. Carolina—Mangum—(our friend) would vote
        with the party if brought on
        now—Brown against us—
S. Carolina *Hayne dead against the Bank*—Miller
        against us *now*. Georgia Forsyth—on
        our side but for this Session would
        be adverse.   Kentucky (Clay)   1
Tennessee—Grundy would work for us strongly *bye and bye*,
        But now would be contra.   Ohio and
        Louisiana   4

. . . .

Alabama—Moore *con.* King—in favor, but would go with
        party if *now* to vote.[14]
Missouri—(Buckner)   1

. . . .

This letter not only represents the point of view of the pro-
Bank democrats as to the inadvisability of raising the Bank issue
in this session but also shows McLane's first estimate of the Senate's vote with seven pro-Bank members expected to vote against
the Bank. This estimate was by no means final, however. For the
next few days Cadwalader devoted himself to consultations with
Secretary McLane, Congressman McDuffie, and General Smith
(United States Senator from Maryland), a staunch supporter of
the Bank and a Democrat, estimating and reestimating to determine as accurately as possible how each member of the Senate

---

[14] King had promised to make his debate in the Senate in favor of the Bank,
yet ultimately voted against the Bank. See Ingersoll to Biddle, March 1, 1932,
NBP.

and House would vote *if the issue were to be brought up during that session*. These men in turn had pro- and anti-Bank congressmen poll their delegates as to their anticipated votes. Cadwalader sifted, refined, and weighed these reports until he was satisfied that he could accurately and confidently report to Biddle exactly how each man would cast his vote.

One need not depend solely on the Biddle Manuscripts for this information. For example, in Cole's *Whig Party in the South* the Mangum Manuscripts are quoted to show why Mangum of North Carolina voted against the Bank even though he was pro-Bank. Congressmen were not the only ones to take this position. John A. Quitman, governor of Mississippi, made the position quite clear. In the summer of 1832, when the question of rechartering the Bank absorbed and agitated the country, the friends of the Bank in Mississippi proposed to waive all other issues and nominate an electoral ticket solely with reference to that question. They announced the names of several men who, as to other leading questions, held different views. Quitman was nominated and he wrote the following letter:

To James Cook

Monmouth, Aug. 28, 1832

On my return from the eastern section of the state, I read in your paper of the 10th inst. an editorial suggestion of the names of several ctizens as electors for President and Vice-President of the United States, who are known to be in favor of a renewal of the charter of the Bank of the United States, with a request that the individuals named should signify to you their acceptance or rejection of the proposed nomination. My name having been suggested, I conceive it a duty to state that, although I have long considered the Bank of the United States a valuable institution, well calculated to promote the general good by its tendency to lessen the price of exchange, and to produce and preserve a uniform and sound paper currency throughout the Union, and would be pleased to see its charter renewed . . . yet, I do not consider the question of rechartering it the *only* [15] or

[15] Italicized words are in italics in the original letter.

most important one which is likely to be involved in the election of the first and second officers of the government. . . . [16]

Then there were important statesmen such as George Dallas, senator from Pennsylvania at the time, who voted pro-Bank in 1832 but after the Veto declared that Jackson was more important than the Bank.[17] We also know from Bassett that "while many politicians nearer home sent assurances of support, James Buchanan, in St. Petersburg, sent in his submission." He was in favor of the Bank, but after the Veto he would support his leader.[18]

But we are primarily interested here in those senators who voted against the Bank before the Veto but who are known actually to have favored the institution. Below is a list of all senators who voted against the institution with an asterisk next to their names if they were supporters of the Bank.[19]

Wm. R. King *	Alabama
Gabriel Moore	Alabama
Geo. M. Troupe	Georgia
John Forsythe *	Georgia
Elias K. Kane *	Illinois
Geo. M. Bibb	Kentucky
Thos. H. Benton	Missouri
Powhatan Ellis *	Mississippi
Isaac Hill	New Hampshire
Mahlon Dickerson *	New Jersey
Chas. Dudley	New York
Wm. Marcy	New York

[16] J. F. H. Claiborne, *Life and Correspondence of John A. Quitman* (2 vols., New York: Harper & Bros., 1860), I, pp. 130–31.

[17] John Spencer Bassett, *The Life of Andrew Jackson* (2 vols., New York: Doubleday, Page and Co., 1911), II, p. 620.

[18] *Ibid.*, p. 621

[19] We are not entirely dependent on the Biddle Papers for this information, although it is probable that the information in the Papers is trustworthy, since it came from members of Jackson's Cabinet or his Kitchen Cabinet who would have no motive for exaggerating. However, see Milton Sydney Heath, *Constructive Liberalism* (Boston: Harvard University Press, 1954), p. 167, on Forsythe, and Arthur Charles Cole, *The Whig Party in the South* (Washington: American Historical Association, 1913), p. 26, on Mangum.

Bedford Brown *	North Carolina
E. P. Mangum *	North Carolina
Robert Hayne	South Carolina
S. D. Miller *	South Carolina
H. L. White	Tennessee
Felix Grundy *	Tennessee
L. W. Tazewell	Virginia
John Tyler	Virginia

Of twenty senators, nine voted contrary to their feelings about the Bank. Is it correct, then, to say as Catterall did, that an analysis of the senatorial vote indicates how the various sections of the country felt about the Bank at the time? Since there are only two senators per state, a change in one vote means a 50 per cent change in the generalization we can make about a particular state. If we analyze the senators in favor of the Bank on this basis,[20] the resulting generalization is that New York and Virginia opposed the Bank, for these are the only two states in which both senators were genuinely opposed to the Bank. Nine of fourteen in the South and Southwest were in favor of it and seventeen of twenty-six, in the South and West. We cannot then say that "the determined opposition was from the South and Southwest." In fact we must conclude that the South, Southwest, and West favored the Bank, a generalization which will appear nearer the truth in subsequent chapters.

Whatever bias was introduced by Catterall into his analysis of the 1832 vote has been greatly reduced by our inclusion of the House of Representatives. We have counted a senatorial vote no more heavily than a representative's vote. Since there were 192 votes cast from the House and 48 from the Senate, the error involved is now considerably less. Furthermore, when the House vote is analyzed in the Biddle Manuscripts as to how it is anticipated the representatives will vote, there is closer agreement between the representatives' real sentiments and their voting behavior than existed in the Senate.

[20] There is no indication that any senator known to be against the Bank actually voted in favor of it.

After the election of 1832 there began a series of vindictive incidents between Jackson and Biddle finally resulting in the removal of the government deposits by Jackson and a contraction of the money supply by Biddle.

In 1834 Polk of Tennessee succeeded in getting the issue of the Bank referred to the House Ways and Means Committee. The Committee offered a resolution on April 4th that the "Bank ought not to be rechartered." On this issue the vote stood at 134 against the Bank and 82 in favor. Although we are not concerned with events after 1832, it is interesting to compare this later vote with that of 1832. (See Map 2, and Table 2, pp. 18–19.)

Contrary, again, to what one would expect, the far western frontier states have grown more favorably disposed toward the Bank than before. The only western state consistently against the Bank was Tennessee, Jackson's home state. As was previously mentioned, Louisiana continued full support. The New England split was more intensified, with Rhode Island undecided. The South remained about as intensely anti-Bank as before. The turnabout in Indiana, Ohio, New Jersey, and Maryland is very dramatic. Pennsylvania should really be included in this category; being the home of the Bank, and passing from 96 per cent favorable to 52 per cent favorable constitutes a comparable change.

When both votes are considered, it appears that consistent support came from Louisiana, Missouri, Kentucky, Delaware, Connecticut, Massachusetts, and Vermont. Consistent anti-Bank states were Tennessee, Alabama, Georgia, South Carolina, North Carolina, Virginia, New York, New Hampshire, and Maine. A neat generalization about either of these groups is hard to come by. Perhaps there is none. It may be that Louisiana had completely different reasons from those of Connecticut for its complete support of the Bank. The problem has always been attacked at the national level. No systematic work has been done to discern the attitude toward the Bank at the state level.

MAP 2

United States House of Representatives Vote, 1834

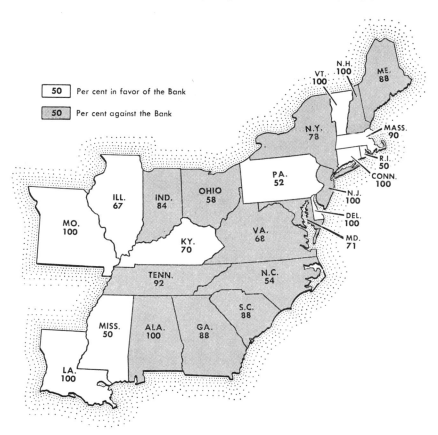

| 50 | Per cent in favor of the Bank |
| 50 | Per cent against the Bank |

TABLE 2

United States House of Representatives Vote, *1834*

State	For	Against	State	For	Against
Maine	1	7	Mississippi	1	1
New Hampshire	0	4	Virginia	6	13
Vermont	5	0	South Carolina	1	7
Connecticut	6	0	Tennessee	1	12
Massachusetts	9	1	North Carolina	6	7
Rhode Island	1	1	Georgia	1	7
New York	7	29	Alabama	0	4
New Jersey	0	5	Louisiana	2	0
Pennsylvania	12	11	Ohio	8	11
Delaware	1	0	Illinois	2	1
Maryland	2	5	Indiana	1	5
Kentucky	7	3	Missouri	2	0

3

New York State Legislators' Support [1]

BECAUSE New York, with some thirty-odd votes to cast in Congress, was such a decisive influence that state seems a likely one to examine in detail. Moreover, subsequent chapters will show New York to be sufficiently complex to warrant its being considered in greater depth than the other states.

Just as the earliest vote in the nation was less politically involved, so was the earliest vote in the New York Assembly. [2] In March of 1831 Assemblyman Morehouse of Otsego County moved the following resolution: "Resolved, that it is the sentiment of this legislature, that the charter of the bank of the United States ought not be renewed." [3] In April the Assembly considered the resolution. It was actively opposed by two New York Jacksonians, Selden and Livingston, and an anti-Mason, J. C. Spencer from Ontario County. After making a speech against the resolution, Selden moved that the resolution be indefinitely postponed. The motion was lost by a vote of 55-55 on April 6th. (See Map 3, and Table 3, pp. 22-23.)

There was very little support of the Bank throughout the eastern part of the state except for New York City. Dutchess County should be discounted somewhat, since only half of its representatives voted. Sullivan, Schoharie, and Schenectady, on the other hand, cast all the votes to which they were entitled in favor of the Bank. Washington County cast two of three votes in favor of the resolution, and Warren cast the only one to

---

[1] For the votes in New York State the *Assembly Journal* and *Senate Journal* were used. *The New York Civil List*, prepared by Franklin B. Hough (Albany: Weed, Parsons & Co., 1851), was used to identify voters' residences.

[2] Jabez Delano Hammond, *The History of Political Parties in the State of New York* (2 vols., New York: H. and E. Phinney, 1846), II, pp. 351-52.

[3] *Ibid.*, p. 351.

which it was entitled the same way. Moving over to the central part of the state, we see that the only clear-cut support came from Broome, Chenango, and Jefferson Counties. Otherwise this part of the state was decidedly anti-Bank. The one region outside New York City to give strong support was the far western area.

On April 9th, just three days after the April 6th vote, the Assembly voted on the resolution not to recharter the Bank. The results were 73–35 against the Bank. (See Map 4, and Table 4, pp. 24–25.) Among the former supporters, thirteen changed their votes and eight failed to vote. This would have made 34 in favor of the Bank, but one vote was picked up in Queens, whose representative had not voted on April 6th. The opponents picked up the thirteen changed votes, nine new votes where there had not been any before, and lost four because of failure to vote.

The changed votes occurred only in the east and central counties—Sullivan, Albany, two in Schoharie, Schenectady, Washington, Warren, Herkimer, St. Lawrence, two in Jefferson, Chenango, and Tioga. Except for New York City and Queens, no county in the central or eastern portions supported the Bank any longer.

New York City did not change any votes. Four previously pro-Bank members failed to vote and two anti-Bank votes were picked up, making the result 4–3 in favor of the Bank. Of a total of eight pro-Bank members throughout the state who failed to vote on the April 9th issue after voting on April 6th, 50 per cent came from New York City which seems more than accidental. Between April 6th and April 9th strong political pressure had been brought to bear, and thirteen members throughout the counties changed their votes. Yet in New York City not one of the eight former pro-Bank members went so far as to change his vote. Four simply did not vote. This suggests that pro-Bank sentiment was sufficiently powerful in the City to encourage resist-

MAP 3
New York State Assembly Vote, April 6, 1831

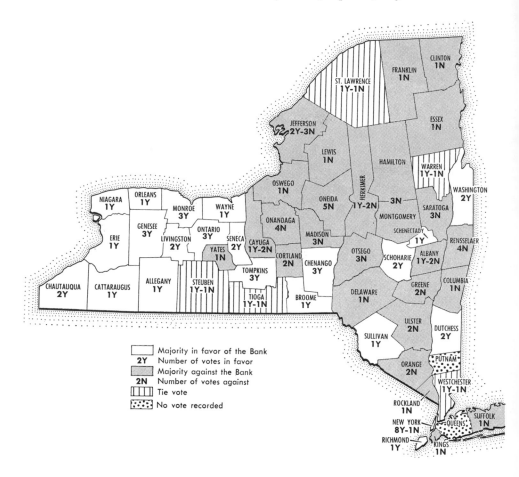

CLINTON 1N

FRANKLIN 1N

ST. LAWRENCE 1Y-1N

JEFFERSON 2Y-3N

ESSEX 1N

LEWIS 1N

HAMILTON

WARREN 1Y-1N

WASHINGTON 2Y

OSWEGO 1N

ONEIDA 5N

HERKIMER 1Y-2N

3N

SARATOGA 3N

MONTGOMERY

NIAGARA 1Y

ORLEANS 1Y

MONROE 3Y

WAYNE 1Y

SCHENECTADY 1Y

RENSSELAER 4N

GENESEE 3Y

ONTARIO 3Y

ONANDAGA 4N

MADISON 3N

ERIE 1Y

LIVINGSTON 2Y

SENECA 2Y

OTSEGO 3N

SCHOHARIE 2Y

ALBANY 1Y-2N

YATES 1N

CAYUGA 1Y-2N

CORTLAND 2N

CHENANGO 3Y

COLUMBIA 1N

CHAUTAUQUA 2Y

CATTARAUGUS 1Y

ALLEGANY 1Y

STEUBEN 1Y-1N

TOMPKINS 3Y

GREENE 2N

TIOGA 1Y-1N

BROOME 1Y

DELAWARE 1N

ULSTER 2N

DUTCHESS 2Y

SULLIVAN 1Y

PUTNAM

ORANGE 2N

WESTCHESTER 1Y-1N

ROCKLAND 1N

NEW YORK 8Y-1N

RICHMOND 1Y

QUEENS

KINGS 1N

SUFFOLK 1N

☐ Majority in favor of the Bank
2Y Number of votes in favor
▨ Majority against the Bank
2N Number of votes against
▥ Tie vote
⣿ No vote recorded

TABLE 3

New York State Assembly Vote, April 6, 1831

County	For	Against	Members Elected	County	For	Against	Members Elected
Albany	1	2	3	Oneida	0	5	5
Allegany	1	0	1	Onondaga	0	4	4
Broome	1	0	1	Ontario	3	0	3
Cattaraugus	1	0	1	Orange	0	2	3
Cayuga	1	2	4	Orleans	1	0	1
Chautauqua	2	0	2	Oswego	0	1	1
Chenango	3	0	3	Otsego	0	3	4
Clinton	0	1	1	Putnam	0	0	1
Columbia	0	1	3	Queens	0	0	1
Cortland	0	2	2	Rensselaer	0	4	4
Delaware	0	1	2	Richmond	1	0	1
Dutchess	2	0	4	Rockland	0	1	1
Erie	1	0	2	Saratoga	0	3	3
Essex	0	1	1	St. Lawrence	1	1	2
Franklin	0	1	1	Schenectady	1	0	1
Genesee	3	0	3	Schoharie	2	0	2
Greene	0	2	2	Seneca	2	0	2
Herkimer	1	2	3	Steuben	1	1	2
Jefferson	2	0	3	Suffolk	0	1	2
Kings	0	1	1	Sullivan	1	0	1
Lewis	0	1	1	Tioga	1	1	2
Livingston	2	0	2	Tompkins	3	0	3
Madison	0	3	3	Ulster	0	2	2
Monroe	3	0	3	Warren	1	0	1
Montgomery and Hamilton	0	3	3	Washington	2	0	3
				Wayne	1	0	2
New York	8	1	11	Westchester	1	1	3
Niagara	1	0	1	Yates	0	1	1

MAP 4
New York State Assembly Vote, April 9, 1831

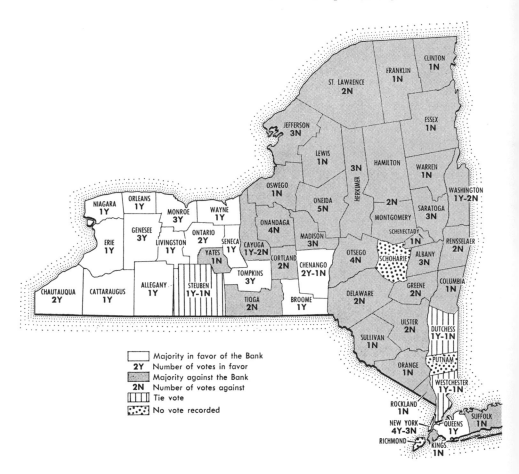

☐	Majority in favor of the Bank
2Y	Number of votes in favor
▦	Majority against the Bank
2N	Number of votes against
⫴	Tie vote
⦙⦙	No vote recorded

TABLE 4

New York State Assembly Vote, April 9, 1831

County	For	Against	Members Elected	County	For	Against	Members Elected
Albany	0	3	3	Oneida	0	5	5
Allegany	1	0	1	Onondaga	0	4	4
Broome	1	0	1	Ontario	3	0	3
Cattaraugus	1	0	1	Orange	0	1	3
Cayuga	1	2	4	Orleans	1	0	1
Chautauqua	2	0	2	Oswego	0	1	1
Chenango	2	1	3	Otsego	0	4	4
Clinton	0	1	1	Putnam	0	0	1
Columbia	0	1	1	Queens	1	0	1
Cortland	0	2	2	Rensselaer	0	2	4
Delaware	0	2	2	Richmond	0	0	1
Dutchess	1	1	4	Rockland	0	1	1
Erie	1	0	2	Saratoga	0	3	3
Essex	0	1	1	St. Lawrence	0	2	2
Franklin	0	1	1	Schenectady	0	1	1
Genesee	3	0	3	Schoharie	0	2	2
Greene	0	2	2	Seneca	1	0	2
Herkimer	0	3	3	Steuben	1	1	2
Jefferson	0	3	3	Suffolk	0	1	2
Kings	0	1	1	Sullivan	0	1	1
Lewis	0	1	1	Tioga	0	2	2
Livingston	1	0	2	Tompkins	3	0	3
Madison	0	3	3	Ulster	0	2	2
Monroe	3	0	3	Warren	0	1	1
Montgomery and Hamilton	0	2	3	Washington	1	2	3
New York	4	3	11	Wayne	1	0	2
Niagara	1	0	1	Westchester	1	1	3
				Yates	0	1	1

ance to the Albany Regency. The New York Senate vote of April 12th, on this resolution adds credence to the argument. Of the three votes cast from the First District, two came from New York City and one from Suffolk County. Both New York City votes were pro-Bank, and one of the senators, Senator Sherman, was a Democrat.

The willingness to resist Democratic pressure should not be underrated. High-ranking politicians such as Gulian Verplanck of New York City and Erastus Root [4] of Delaware County were barred by the Regency, the group of politicians led by Martin Van Buren who directed Democratic Party strategy in New York, from holding further political office because they supported the Bank. A Democrat paid a high price for supporting his conviction by casting a pro-Bank vote in New York. New York City must have entertained very positive feeling for the Bank in order for its democratic legislators to defy the Regency.

New York State Senatorial Vote, April 12, 1831

	Pro-Bank	Anti-Bank
First District (Kings, Queens, Richmond, Suffolk, New York)	2	1
Second District (Dutchess, Putnam, Rockland, Orange, Sullivan, Ulster, Westchester)	0	3
Third District (Albany, Columbia, Greene, Rensselaer, Schenectady, Schoharie)	0	4
Fourth District (Clinton, Essex, Franklin, Hamilton, Montgomery, St. Lawrence, Saratoga, Warren, Washington)	1	3
Fifth District	2	2

[4] Bray Hammond, *Banks and Politics in America* (Princeton: Princeton University Press, 1957), pp. 362, 393.

	Pro-Bank	Anti-Bank
(Herkimer, Jefferson, Lewis, Madison, Oneida, Oswego)		
Sixth District	1	2
(Broome, Chenango, Cortland, Delaware, Otsego, Tioga, Tompkins)		
Seventh District	2	2
(Cayuga, Onondaga, Ontario, Seneca, Wayne, Yates)		
Eighth District	4	0
(Allegany, Cattaraugus, Chautauqua, Erie, Genesee, Livingston, Monroe, Niagara, Orleans, Steuben)		

The 1832 and 1834 votes in the House of Representatives by New York congressmen may be seen as analogous to the state vote. The New York congressional districts were based on counties, but some districts included more than one county. Inasmuch as there were some changes in these districts between 1832 and 1834, a vote by a member of the House of Representatives is shown only in the county in which he resided. For example, if Sullivan and Ulster Counties constituted one congressional district and the congressman's residence was Ulster, his vote is shown in Ulster County only. The New York State senatorial vote is handled the same way. This method could not have been adopted had there been subtle fluctuations from county to county. Fortunately the voting was very uniform throughout each section of the state. When these votes are added, in the manner indicated, to the two State Assembly votes, the results are those shown on Map 5. (See Map 5 and Table 5, pp. 28–29.)

The far western support of the Bank was unequivocal. The most developed section of the United States, New York City, showed good support. Except for Broome, Chenango, and Washington Counties, the rest of the state was against the bank.

The most surprising conclusion to be drawn from the evi-

MAP 5

Five Crucial Votes in New York State, 1831–1834

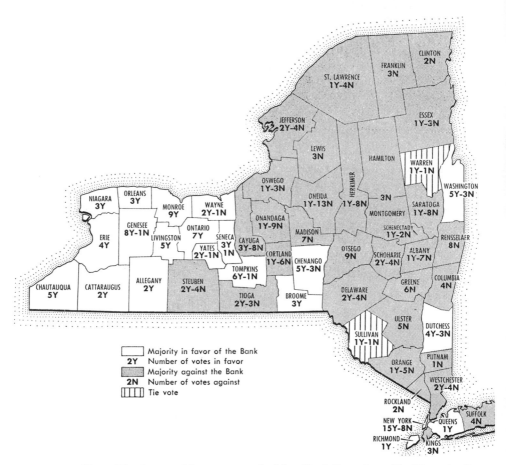

Majority in favor of the Bank
2Y Number of votes in favor
Majority against the Bank
2N Number of votes against
Tie vote

Note: The five crucial votes were the New York State Assembly Vote, April 6, 1831 (see Map 3, and Table 3); New York State Assembly Vote, April 9, 1831 (see Map 4, and Table 4); New York State Senate Vote, April 12, 1831 (see pp. 26–27); United States House of Representatives Vote from New York State, 1832 (see Map 1, and Table 1); United States House of Representatives Vote from New York State, 1834 (see Map 2, and Table 2).

TABLE 5
Five Crucial Votes in New York State, 1831–1834

County	N.Y. Assembly 4/6/31		N.Y. Assembly 4/9/31		N.Y. Senate 4/12/31		U.S. House 1832		U.S. House 1834	
	For	Against	For	Against	For	Against	For	Against	For	Against
Albany	1	2	0	3			0	1	0	1
Allegany	1	0	1	0						
Broome	1	0	1	0			1	0		
Cattaraugus	1	0	1	0	1	0				
Cayuga	1	2	1	2	1	1	0	1	0	1
Chautauqua	2	0	2	0					1	0
Chenango	3	0	2	1	0	1	1	0	0	1
Clinton	0	1	0	1						
Columbia	0	1	0	1			0	1	0	1
Cortland	0	2	0	2	1	0	0	1	0	1
Delaware	0	1	0	2	1	0	1	0	0	1
Dutchess	2	0	1	1	0	1	1	0	0	1
Erie	1	0	1	0	1	0			1	0
Essex	0	1	0	1	1	0			0	1
Franklin	0	1	0	1			0	1		
Genesee	3	0	3	0	1	0	1	0	0	1
Greene	0	2	0	2	0	1			0	1
Herkimer	1	2	0	3	0	1	0	1	0	1
Jefferson	2	0	0	3			0	1	0	1
Kings	0	1	0	1			0	1		
Lewis	0	1	0	1			0	1		
Livingston	2	0	1	0	1	0			1	0
Madison	0	3	0	3					0	1
Monroe	3	0	3	0			1	0	1	0
Montgomery and Hamilton	0	3	0	2	0	1	0	1	0	1
New York	8	1	4	3	2	0	1	2	0	2
Niagara	1	0	1	0			1	0		
Oneida	0	5	0	5	1	1	0	1	0	1
Onondaga	0	4	0	4	1	0			0	1
Ontario	3	0	3	0					1	0
Orange	0	2	0	1	0	1	1	0	0	1
Orleans	1	0	1	0					0	1
Oswego	0	1	0	1	1	0			0	1
Otsego	0	3	0	4	0	1			0	1
Putnam	0	0	0	0	0	1				
Queens	0	0	1	0						

TABLE 5 *continued*
Accumulated Vote

County	N.Y. Assembly 4/6/31		N.Y. Assembly 4/9/31		N.Y. Senate 4/12/31		U.S. House 1832		U.S. House 1834	
	For	Against	For	Against	For	Against	For	Against	For	Against
Rensselaer	0	4	0	2			0	1	0	1
Richmond	1	0	0	0						
Rockland	0	1	0	1						
Saratoga	0	3	0	3	0	1	1	0	0	1
St. Lawrence	1	1	0	2					0	1
Schenectady	1	0	0	1	0	1				
Schoharie	2	0	0	2	0	1	0	1		
Seneca	2	0	1	0	0	1				
Steuben	1	1	1	1			0	1	0	1
Suffolk	0	1	0	1	0	1			0	1
Sullivan	1	0	0	1						
Tioga	1	1	0	2			1	0		
Tompkins	3	0	3	0					0	1
Ulster	0	2	0	2			0	1		
Warren	1	0	0	1						
Washington	2	0	1	2	0	1	1	0	1	0
Wayne	1	0	1	0	0	1				
Westchester	1	1	1	1			0	1	0	1
Yates	0	1	0	1			1	0		

dence taken as a whole is that at both the national and the New York state level the legislators of the West supported the Bank. This sufficiently contradicts traditional thinking to warrant focusing attention on another conventionally accepted concept, namely, state bank hostility to the Second United States Bank, sometimes believed to have been most intense in the South and West.

4

State Bank Support of the Second Bank

NO EXPLANATION of the influences working for the destruction of the second United States Bank has had wider acceptance or a longer history than the theory of the state banks' hostility to the Bank. Jabez Hammond considered this hostility to be caused by the state banks' greed for the deposits of the United States government:

The state banks believed, that if the United States Bank should be annihilated, these immense deposits would be made in their own vaults, and hence all the benefits arising from these deposits, and also the whole profits of the very great circulation of the United States Bank notes would be transferred from the United States to the state banks, without compelling them to increase their own capital to the amount of a single dollar. Was it in human nature, and especially, was it in *bank nature*, (if such an expression may be tolerated,) to resist this prospect of adding to their gains? [1]

Catterall accepted the notion of the state banks' hostility, but explained it in these terms: "The opposition of state banks whose interests were involved arrayed a powerful party against the bank. It had forced many of them to restrict their business by compelling payment for their notes in specie, and it had been particularly active and particularly offensive in this in the South and West." [2] He went on to add that the profits of state banks were reduced because the Bank loaned at 6 per cent, being compelled to do so by its charter, whereas the state banks could have loaned at 7 per cent had they not been forced to loan at the lower rate "because the big bank did so."

[1] Jabez Delano Hammond, *The History of Political Parties in the State of New York* (2 vols., New York: H. and E. Phinney, 1846), II, 350.
[2] Ralph C. H. Catterall, *The Second Bank of the United States* (Chicago: University of Chicago Press, 1903), p. 166.

Present day writers have accepted the existence of state banks' hostility as a very powerful force against the Bank and have used some combination of causes derived from the earlier writers to support their views. Govan is an exception to this generalization. Although his interest was not centered around the identification of the friends and enemies of the Bank, he noted that state banks ceased complaining against the Bank and he mentioned several state banks that were in favor of the Second Bank.[3]

In the face of almost universal consensus it might seem odd to be investigating support of the Bank in the area of the state banks. However, Bassett, referring to the time, January 1832, when the Bank sent its memorial to Congress requesting renewal of its charter, remarked: "Petitions were secured in large numbers, the most notable being from banks and business organizations in favor of the bank."[4] One is compelled to ask why the most notable petitions should come from state banks if they were hostile? Nicholas Biddle, who was in a very good position to know, does not seem to have believed in the theory.

January 16, 1832

Jeramiah Mason, Esq.[5]
Portsmouth, N. H.

. . . It would be very useful if your community and especially your banks would aid us, for we should then disarm the enemies of the institution of one of their most efficient weapons, the imaginary injury done to the State Banks, and the jealousy which they are presumed to feel toward the institution. . . .[6]

February 27, 1832

Honble. H. Seymour[7]
Wash., D. C.

. . . I do not care about this, the object being to multiply the

[3] Thomas Payne Govan, *Nicholas Biddle, Nationalist and Public Banker, 1786–1844* (Chicago: University of Chicago Press, 1959), pp. 85, 176.
[4] John Spencer Bassett, *The Life of Andrew Jackson* (2 vols., New York: Doubleday, Page & Co., 1911), II, 615.
[5] President of the United States branch bank at Portsmouth.
[6] Biddle to Mason, January 16, 1832, in the President's Letter Books (Manuscript Division, Library of Congress, Washington, D.C.). Cited hereafter as PLB.
[7] United States Senator from Vermont.

proofs that the State Banks are in the main friendly to his institution.[8]

These letters show that Biddle was aware of the accusation that the state banks were hostile but that he disbelieved it. It appeared to him to be propaganda, resting on an imaginary base, spread by the Bank's enemies. Moreover, he was so sure of his convictions that he was willing to try to prove that "state banks are in the main friendly."

In attempting to locate support among the state banks, one naturally ought to begin by finding the areas in which Biddle hoped for support. In January of 1832 Biddle weighed two conflicting sets of advice: Members of Jackson's cabinet advised not petitioning for renewal of the charter that session of Congress; while Webster, Clay, and the Bank's lobbyists in Washington, Horace Binney and Thomas Cadwalader,[9] advised proceeding with the renewal request immediately. He decided in favor of the latter course. The petition was to be presented in the House of Representatives by George McDuffie of South Carolina and in the Senate by Dallas of Pennsylvania, both Democrats. Although Biddle had previously been informed of a pro-Bank majority in both Houses, he felt the need to rally the Bank's friends throughout the Union. As a result on January 16, 1832, he began a series of letters addressed mainly to officers of the branches of the Bank requesting that memorials be sent to Congress from citizens, from state banks, from state legislatures. To some areas he wrote only for memorials from citizens. To others, he wrote for state bank memorials and citizens' memorials. To still other areas he also asked for the state legislatures to pass resolutions and forward them to Congress. The extent of help asked for and the tone of the letters indicate the areas in which Biddle felt he had reason to hope for state bank support.

The answers he received reveal a great deal of information as to the attitudes of state banks in various sections of the country.

[8] PLB, February 27, 1832.
[9] Both were directors on the Philadelphia Board of the Bank.

Finally, the memorials of state banks actually recorded as presented in Congress provide the strongest and most clear-cut evidence of support.

Using these letters and memorials as basic materials, let us see what they reveal about the attitudes of state banks just prior to the 1832 Veto. Because these letters and memorials were so important, we will paraphrase them in the present tense and will try to be as faithful to the 1832 style of writing as we can.

Since the Bank is thought of as having been especially offensive to the state banks in the West and South, these sections will be examined first. To no one did Biddle write with greater confidence of success than to Samuel Jaudon, cashier of the New Orleans branch of the Bank. Though he recognizes that the New Orleans delegation to congress is pro-Bank, he asks that memorials from the citizens and the state banks be sent along.[10] On February 11, 1832, Jaudon answered that the memorial from the Louisiana State Bank has been adopted unanimously. He will furnish one for the Bank of Orleans and it will be passed. During the week he hopes all banks will sign.[11] A few days later he wrote again to say the Bank of Orleans has sent a memorial and that the Canal Bank has appointed a committee to do the same. At the next meeting of the Bank of Louisiana, the question will be brought up there.

According to congressional records, memorials from the Louisiana State Bank,[12] the New Orleans Bank,[13] the New Orleans Canal and Banking Company,[14] and the Bank of Orleans [15] were presented in Congress. What proportion of the state banks in Louisiana did this represent?

Up to 1832 Knox referred to only two banks in Louisiana, the Louisiana State Bank and the Bank of Louisiana.[16] Jaudon

---

[10] Biddle to Jaudon, January 16, 1832, PLB.
[11] Jaudon to Biddle, February 11, 1832, NBP.
[12] *House Journal*, 22nd Congress, 1st Session, p. 450.   [13] *Ibid.*, p. 534.
[14] *Senate Documents*, 22nd Congress, 1st Session, vol. II, doc. 108.
[15] *Executive Documents*, 22nd Congress, 1st Session, vol. IV, doc. 187.
[16] John J. Knox, *A History of Banking in the United States* (New York: B. Rhodes and Co., 1900), p. 611.

wrote of "all" banks and specified three. Despite this discrepancy, it seems safe to conclude that the state banks of Louisiana were clearly pro-Bank. Their economic reasons for so feeling are contained in the memorials, and these, along with those from other states, will be examined later. The task for the moment will be to locate the areas of state bank support or hostility as the case may be.

Turning to Louisiana's neighbor to the east, Mississippi, there appears to be no evidence of antagonism there. In 1809 the Bank of Mississippi at Natchez was chartered as a private institution. In 1818 the Legislature extended its powers, and it became a state bank. This new charter was to continue until 1840, up to which time no other bank was to be chartered. This bank appears to have been successful and well managed, but the Legislature, disregarding its previous pledge, established in 1830 the Planter's Bank of Mississippi, and made it the state financial agent. "The managers of the Bank of the State of Mississippi, dreading the evils which they feared would result from speculation in negroes and wild land, then so prevalent, concluded to wind up that institution." [17] From this we deduce that in 1832 there were at most two state banks, the Planter's and the Bank of Mississippi.

Biddle wrote Wilkins, president of the branch in Natchez, for either citizens' memorials or state bank memorials. Both the Planter's Bank and the Bank of the State of Mississippi sent Congress memorials; Mississippi's state banks thus gave full support.[18]

Missouri's supposed state bank hostility can be quickly disposed of. Biddle in writing John O'Fallon, president of the United States branch in St. Louis, fails to ask for memorials from the state banks but requests an expression from the state legislature only.[19] This is not strange, since there were no state banks

[17] Knox, p. 602.
[18] *House Journal*, 22nd Congress, 1st Session, p. 510.
[19] Biddle to O'Fallon, January 16, 1832, PLB.

EDWARD MINER GALLAUDET MEMORIAL LIBRARY
GALLAUDET COLLEGE
WASHINGTON, D. C.   99928

in Missouri at the time. "The disappearance of the two pioneer
banks left the chief town in Missouri, now with a population of
4,500 and a growing trade, without any banking facilities, . . .
and this condition of things lasted until 1829, when the United
States Bank opened a branch at St. Louis. . . ." The next bank
to be chartered was in 1837.[20]

Illinois, lying between Missouri and Indiana, had no branch
bank of the United States. Hence there is no correspondence in
the Biddle Papers concerning the attitude of the state banks.
Knox told us that Illinois had at most one bankrupt state bank;
indeed, as late as 1835 there were only two banks in existence
with a total circulation of $178,810.[21]

Similarly, Indiana had no branch of the Bank. But Knox
pointed out "the collapse of the bank ended banking business in
the State, so far as banks of issue were concerned, with the exception of the Farmers' and Mechanics' Bank, at Madison, which
maintained its credit, and on the expiration of its charter was au-
thorized by the Legislature to continue business until 1834,
when the State Bank was chartered." [22] Indiana then need not
concern us here any more than Illinois.

Biddle wrote Herman Cope, president of the Bank in Cincinnati, for an expression from its citizens and state banks.[23] Cope
answered on February 4, 1832, that the Board of Directors of
the Commercial Bank of Cincinnati will pass a favorable memorial. He went on to say that most, if not all, the state banks in
Ohio will do the same.[24] As listed in the several records of Congress, memorials were received from the Commercial Bank of
Cincinnati, the Bank of St. Clairsville, the Bank of Steubens-
ville,[25] and the Farmers' and Mechanics' Bank of Steubens-
ville.[26]

---

[20] Knox, pp. 712–18.   [21] Ibid., p. 729.   [22] Ibid., p. 694.
[23] Biddle to Cope, January 16, 1832, PLB.
[24] Cope to Biddle, February 4, 1832, NBP.
[25] House Journal, 22nd Congress, 1st Session, pp. 408, 413, 474.
[26] Executive Documents, 22nd Congress, 1st Session, vol. IV, doc. 167

Just exactly how many banks existed in Ohio at the time is hard to tell. Judging from Knox one might hazard a guess of thirteen. However, it is clear from the memorial from the Commercial Bank of Cincinnati that outside of the Commercial Bank, whose capital was $500,000, the other banks were rather insignificant. Similarly a memorial from the citizens of Louisville, Kentucky, states that Kentucky, Indiana, Illinois, Missouri, and Tennessee have no banking institutions of their own and that Ohio and Alabama have none of extended credit.[27] Since the most important state bank, as well as three others, gave positive support to the Bank, it is fair to conclude that the Ohio state banks supported the institution. This will become even clearer when other memorials are examined.

There was a branch of the Bank at Louisville, Kentucky. Biddle asks John Tilford "will your fellow citizens aid?"[28] Why he asked for no help from the state banks is evident; none existed there.[29] According to Knox, "After the liquidation of the Bank of Kentucky and the Bank of the Commonwealth of Kentucky, the State had to depend for paper money on the notes of the branches of the Bank of the United States at Lexington and Louisville, and the bills of banks located outside its borders."[30] Not until 1833–1834 were any state banks chartered. Again, during this period, state bank hostility was obviously not to be found in Kentucky.

There is no correspondence from Nicholas Biddle to the branch in Nashville requesting supporting memorials. But as late as 1834 only one state bank was reported for Tennessee.[31] Since this was Andrew Jackson's home state, perhaps Biddle wisely hesitated from asking legislative aid or memorials from citizens. Jackson, incidentally, was known to have kept his own banking account with the Nashville branch of the Bank. Had there been

---

[27] *Ibid.*, vol. IV, doc. 111.   [28] Biddle to Tilford, January 16, 1832, PLB.
[29] We know from the previously mentioned memorial of the citizens of Louisville that this situation in Kentucky was also one of no existing state banks.
[30] Knox, pp. 634–35.   [31] *Ibid.*, p. 667.

a state bank at the time, one would think—given Jackson's attitude toward the Bank—that his money would have been deposited with the state bank.

Turning to the southern states: Alabama is a particularly interesting refutation of the theory that the more "loosely run" state banks were the most hostile to the Bank, especially resenting its restraining hand. After two territorially chartered banks had failed, leaving only the Bank of Mobile, the state legislature enacted a law in 1820 to establish the Bank of the State of Alabama. This bank failed, but in 1823 the state legislature chartered another of the same name. Alabama was so short of gold and silver that the capital of the bank, on which no limit was imposed, was to be furnished by the credit of the state itself. The State General Assembly elected the president and directors. The bank issued all denominations of notes including shinplasters. The loans made were by law apportioned among the several counties. The way for constituents to get loans was through their legislator, and no director of the bank could hope to be reappointed unless he granted whatever loans the legislators requested. Two amusing stories are told to illustrate the situation. A member of the State House of Representatives died, and the other members, as was the custom, wore crepe on their sleeves for thirty days. This indicated to the bank directors the men to be wined and dined. A backwoodsman, observing this, put on a black crepe band and was royally feasted for several days before his identity became known.

The other story concerns a group of hotel keepers in Tuscaloosa and their relation to banking. One hotel keeper, believing that if he were a director of the bank the popularity of his hotel would increase, had himself appointed to the post. At once his hotel was crowded. Perceiving this the other hotel keepers, in order to be competitive, also had themselves appointed as directors. One morning when John L. Tindall, president of the bank, was presiding at a meeting of the directors (most of whom were hotel keepers), a large number of bills were discounted. A small one was offered and no one knew the maker. It was about to be rejected when Tindall, looking at each of the hotel keepers in turn and getting no response from them, remarked quietly, "This man must have camped out last night." [32]

Since times were prosperous between 1826 and 1836 and people had little difficulty in getting all the money they needed, we have, then, the typical agrarian community with the state bank overextended and corrupt. It ought to have hated the Bank, but the very opposite was true, as the following correspondence shows.

On January 16, 1832, Biddle wrote two letters to Alabama requesting help. One was to James Jackson of Tuscaloosa and the other to George Poe, cashier of the branch of the Bank in Mobile. He reminds the former of the good will manifested toward the Bank the previous winter by the Alabama state joint committee reporting on the Bank of Alabama and asks for just such an expression of good will by means of a private memorial or any communication of Jackson's own views to Alabama's delegation in Congress.[33] To the latter, George Poe, he wrote that probably Poe's community and perhaps the banks might be disposed to cooperate. He also asks that the legislature act by sending information to the delegates in Congress.[34]

In response, James Jackson wrote that he is sending Biddle two printed copies of the report of the joint committee of the state legislature on the state and condition of the Bank of the State of Alabama, because of the way in which that report spoke of the branch of the Bank at Mobile. It shows the change of opinion (from a hostile attitude to one of good will) in Alabama on the subject of the Bank.[35]

Poe answered and enclosed a copy of a letter he has written to Tindall, president of the state bank of Alabama. It reports that the Bank of Mobile has passed resolutions expressive of a wish to

[32] Both these stories are in Knox, pp. 598–99.
[33] Biddle to Jackson, January 16, 1832, PLB.
[34] Biddle to Poe, January 16, 1832, PLB.
[35] Jackson to Biddle, January 30, 1832, NBP.

see the charter of the Bank renewed. Tindall had once said that his entire board felt the Bank was of great use to the state bank and that if renewal of the charter depended on his board, it would be renewed. If this is still so, an expression of that opinion in the form of a resolution or by information sent to Congress from the State will be very acceptable as testimony to the administration of the concerns of the Bank in that quarter. The state bank at Tuscaloosa has paid the Bank and the branches with which the state bank has had intercourse a handsome compliment. No state bank has derived more extensive and substantial benefits from the Bank than Mr. Tindall's. Will he please write and say so? [36]

Poe wrote again to Biddle on February 23rd and enclosed a memorial from the Bank of the State of Alabama. He reports that every member of the board of the state bank wants the Bank rechartered.[37] Besides this memorial, the congressional records show that the Bank of Mobile, chartered when Alabama was still a territory, also forwarded one.[38] We can conclude confidently from the above evidence that the banks of Alabama gave the Bank full support.

Strangely, Georgia, immediately to the east of Alabama, showed strong and long-lasting state bank hostility. On January 16th Biddle wrote to John Cumming, president of the branch in Savannah, asking whether the community and state banks will cooperate. He is encouraged to think this because of the failure of the proscriptive measure in the state legislature the previous winter. (See p. 60 and footnote 32, p. 60 for a description of this measure.) It shows decreasing hostility. But he concludes that he will take any kind of help Cumming can get.[39] Cumming answered on January 27th that he and Mr. Hunter, cashier of the

---

[36] Poe to Biddle, February 11, 1832, NBP.
[37] Poe to Biddle, February 23, 1832, NBP.
[38] *Senate Journal*, 22nd Congress, 1st Session, p. 143.
[39] Biddle to Cumming, January 16, 1832, PLB.

branch in Savannah, agree that a memorial will be bad because there are very few friends of the Bank there, and the political leaders are to a man opposed. If a memorial is started a counter-memorial to Congress will be started at once. Among the signers will be public men and stockholders and officers of the local banks. Feeling that he and Hunter might be wrong, they have consulted friends of the Bank, but the latter have all agreed with them.[40]

Thus Georgia is the one state where there is strong evidence of state bank hostility. Knox said that until 1810 only branches of the Bank existed there. Progress in the state was not particularly noticeable: While other states were building cities, promoting manufactures, and building roads and canals, Georgia made few material gains from 1800 to 1810. People consequently grew dissatisfied with the Bank and wanted their own state banks free of federal control.[41]

State banks and the Bank seem to have been in continual conflict in Georgia from 1817 on. The Bank tried to compel specie payment and the state banks resisted through any scheme available. Bills of the state banks were protested, but since the sentiment in Georgia was with the home banks the Bank was unable to retain counsel in Georgia to press its claims. The legislature passed an act in 1820 repealing enough of the law providing for resumption of specie payments so that the law would not apply to a refusal of specie to the Bank by the chartered banks of the state. Hostile legislation continued to be passed as late as 1826.[42] The hostility in 1832 against the Bank has been attributed primarily to loyalty to Jackson, whose Indian policy was universally popular in Georgia and to the fact that it meant political defeat to any politician who opposed Jackson.[43] The congressional records show no memorials as having been received from Georgia.

[40] Cumming to Biddle, January 27, 1832, NBP.
[41] Knox, p. 572.   [42] Ibid., p. 576.   [43] Govan, p. 176.

Neither do the congressional records show any state bank memorials received from South Carolina, but this should not necessarily be interpreted as hostility. Actually the correspondence indicates an awareness on the part of the state banks of the value of the Bank, but fear forces them not to act as a body. James Johnson, president of the Charleston branch, is asked by Biddle for both citizens' and state banks' memorials. He is urged to consult Mr. Alexander and Mr. Pringle, directors of the Charleston branch.[44] Johnson responds that the banks as such will not send memorials for fear of a counterattack but that the directors of the banks as individuals will sign. If George McDuffie will emphasize the economic advantages of the United States Bank, it will make things much easier.[45]

Biddle also wrote to his friend John Potter, formerly of South Carolina but then living in New Jersey, to write and stir up Hayne and some of his old friends in South Carolina.[46] Potter answered on January 25th and enclosed a letter from Mr. Alexander. He is against the Bank. This so mortified Potter that he exclaims, "To what lengths the democrats will go!" He asks what state has benefited more than South Carolina from the Bank. Alexander claims that there could be a memorial from the citizens, but they fear a countermove. Not one state bank has the courage—(here a phrase is illegible) even though they know the advantages of the United States Bank.[47]

Knox said that the Bank started in South Carolina at the same time the first state bank was chartered:

It did a profitable business in sterling and domestic exchange. . . . At the close of the Branch Bank of the United States there arose the necessity of a bank with a large capital to take the place of the Branch Bank. The old banks in Charleston had not accustomed themselves to handling, to any extent foreign exchange; they were very conserva-

[44] Biddle to Johnson, January 16, 1832, PLB.
[45] Johnson to Biddle, January 23, 1832, NBP.
[46] Biddle to Potter, January 16, 1832, PLB.
[47] Potter to Biddle, January 25, 1832, NBP.

tive in their business. The great staples for Carolina of cotton and rice were chiefly sold for foreign exchange.[48]

It would appear from this that the function of the Bank and the state banks differed sufficiently as not to have caused friction. However, in the absence of any positive evidence either for support or hostility, South Carolina will have to remain an unknown.[49]

Apparently Biddle made a special effort to stabilize the currency in North Carolina. One would therefore expect the state banks there to have been especially hostile because of the restraining hand of the Bank which had to be used to bring the local note issues in line. Just the opposite was true. Here again Biddle's letter to John Huske, president of the Fayetteville branch, shows that *because* the Bank stabilized the currency, there should have been support of the Bank in North Carolina—just the opposite to the now prevalent theory.[50] Biddle asks for memorials from citizens, but more especially state bank memorials.

He also wrote Browne, a friend of the Bank in Raleigh, stating that there is a great diversity among the delegates in Congress. This he regrets. He has taken great trouble to try to bring a healthy condition to the currency in North Carolina. Could an expression from citizens, state banks, or the legislature be had? [51]

There were three state banks in the state at that time, the State Bank, the Cape Fear Bank, and the Bank at Newbern.[52] The first and last mentioned sent petitions for renewal to Congress.[53] The contents definitely challenge the theory that those state banks disciplined by the Bank were the most hostile. An addi-

---

[48] Knox, p. 566.

[49] In *The History of the Banking Institutions Organized in South Carolina Prior to 1860* (Columbia: State Co., 1922) by Washington Augustus Clark, there is no reference to any hostility on the part of state banks towards the United States Bank.

[50] Biddle to Huske, January 16, 1832, PLB.

[51] Biddle to Browne, February 27, 1832, PLB.   [52] Knox, p. 550.

[53] *Executive Documents,* 22nd Congress, 1st Session, vol. IV, doc. 166.

tional reason for not being hostile was that the Bank of Cape Fear and the State Bank both owned stock in the Bank. The State Bank claimed $214,000 of specie of which $140,000 was in stock of the Bank on which the state bank drew interest.

Information about the relation between the state banks and the Bank in Virginia, the last southern state to be considered, is limited. In 1832 there were four mother banks together with their branches scattered throughout Virginia and what later became West Virginia. Knox reported very favorably on the adequacy of this system of banking.[54]

There were two branches of the Bank in Virginia, one in Richmond and the other in Norfolk. Biddle in writing R. Anderson, president of the Richmond branch, says that the Bank of Virginia (one of the four mother banks) has in its public reports borne very kindly testimony in favor of the Bank and might be disposed to assist the Bank on this occasion.[55] It is clear from this letter that state bank support was the *only* sort of help Biddle thought possible from Virginia. He continues to Anderson, "I am not I confess sanguine, for between the ultra-constitutionalist, and those who are personally interested, there is a very small space for our friends." Again in writing to George Newton, president of the Norfolk branch, for aid, he says, "I am not sanguine of aid from Virginia, but if any could be obtained, ..."[56]

Records show only one memorial sent to Congress, and that from another parent bank, the Northwestern Bank at Wheeling with branches at Wellsburg, Parkersburg, and Jeffersonville—all situated in the western part of Virginia.[57] This indicates that we might claim 50 per cent support, two out of four parent banks.

To sum up: In the whole South and West only one state, Georgia, can be recognized as clearly evincing strong state bank

[54] Knox, p. 550.   [55] Biddle to Anderson, January 16, 1832, PLB.
[56] Biddle to Newton, January 16, 1832, PLB.
[57] *House Journal*, 22nd Congress, 1st Session, p. 385.

hostility. On the other hand, the banks of Louisiana, Mississpppi, Alabama, North Carolina, and Ohio were active supporters of the Bank, offering between two-thirds and 100 per cent state bank support. We conclude, then, that we must not think of the banks of the South and West as being especially hostile, but that among existing state banks of that area, a heavy majority gave the Bank active support. To add credence to this conclusion, let us now try to discover why the South and West behaved as they did.

5

Economic Reasons for Support

NOT ALL the state bank memorials are printed in the congressional records. Fortunately, however, some do exist for Louisiana, North Carolina, Mississippi, and Ohio, so that we can form an idea of the southwestern, western, and southern points of view. No state banks existed in the far West. A few of the citizens' memorials which are in print, however, may be helpful in judging sentiment from that area. Louisiana is most fully represented with three printed petitions. The Louisiana State Bank and the Bank of Orleans sent identical memorials.[1]

After referring, as almost all the memorials do, to the advantages of a sound currency brought about by the United States Bank, and to the courtesy and liberality with which the state banks in Louisiana and the adjoining states have been treated, they observe with praise that the United States Bank has been able to reduce the rates of exchange below the cost of transporting specie. The Southwest and the West have also benefited in the development of their resources by the Bank's lending to planters, merchants, and mechanics. But New Orleans has received a special benefit: Its position as the connecting link between the commerce of the North and West, and as the only seaport through which foreign trade can be carried on, means that its money transactions are enormous. Sales of produce for export to the North or to foreign ports and the purchase of supplies for the West are mainly paid for by bills of exchange. These find a ready purchaser in the United States Bank branch in New Orleans at a favorable rate. Bills of exchange, then, drawn on all Atlantic cities and Europe, can be disposed of so easily as to promote the spirit

[1] *Executive Documents*, 22nd Congress, 1st Session, vol. IV, doc. 153 and 187.

of enterprise, encourage competition, and secure to the western traders and local planters the highest prices for their products.

Also, according to the memorial, the merchants and planters from the interior are enabled to purchase their supplies in New Orleans by bills of exchange drawn on the various cities of the West nearest their residences. This is made possible because of the Bank's system of branches. Finally, the Bank's ability to get foreign money, something the local banks cannot do, is very important since capital is relatively scarce in Louisiana and the adjoining states.

The memorial of the New Orleans Canal and Banking Company [2] stresses the great harm that will result from the withdrawal of the capital from the West in the event of the Bank's not being rechartered. Agriculture, commerce, and manufacturing will be ruined. Westerners on their own individual responsibility, it goes on to assert, cannot get loans from the East; only through the medium of the Bank can they get the use of surplus capital from the East. Since the Bank has an average of 10 million dollars invested in exchange and discounts there, the citizens of New Orleans will be greatly hurt if this is withdrawn. Interest on money, moreover, has been reduced from 10 or 12 per cent to 6 or 8 per cent, and the rate of exchange on eastern cities from a premium of 5 per cent to a premium of 1½ per cent. The memorial mentions, finally, the benefits of a sound currency.

The Commercial Bank of Cincinnati asserts in its memorial that it has a capital of $500,000. It is the only chartered bank in that city and is the largest in the state. A branch of the Bank with a liberal capital allowance has been in Cincinnati for some time. Its notes and those of the other branches of the Bank constitute the only currency in the western states.

If these state banks were thinking of their interests in only the narrowest sense, they would presumably desire the removal of

[2] *Senate Documents*, 22nd Congress, 1st Session, vol. II, doc. 108.

such a competitor. But they were governed, they say, by motivations of a wider scope.

First, the Bank furnishes a large part of western capital, which is an addition to their own resources. The demise of the Bank would doubtless cause local banks to multiply, but there would be little or no increase of capital since the only capital would be that which is already there. Its withdrawal, therefore, would produce great injury; it would shock the mercantile interests, cause widespread bankruptcy, and depress real estate.

Second, the Bank has given the West a sound currency. A want of this had been felt worst there. The local banks, too numerous and founded on insufficient capital, left the West in a weakened condition [following the Panic of 1819]. Suffering and loss has been extreme in the whole Ohio Valley. Now, however, this region has emerged and is growing prosperous—thanks to the Bank.

Third, the value of the Bank acting to check the excess issues of the local banks is appreciated. The local banks do not have enough capital to supply.

Finally, competition between the Bank and the local banks creates a healthy state of affairs. It keeps the Bank from becoming a monopoly and keeps the local banks from excesses and speculations.[3]

Common to all three memorials, and foremost in them, is the stress laid on the extra capital introduced into the Southwest and West by the Bank and the areas almost sole dependence on the Bank for its currency. The amount of notes of the Bank in circulation in the South and West as of April 4, 1832, in comparison to the total state bank circulation in each of the states as of either 1834 or 1835 (depending on which year statistics are available) supports the state banks' point of view. Since the state note expansion after the Veto of 1832 was very rapid, it is an

---

[3] *Senate Documents*, 22nd Congress, 1st Session, vol. II, doc. 68.

understatement to say that except for Virginia, Georgia, and Ohio, United States Bank notes represented 50 to 100 per cent of the total circulation of state bank notes.

Comparative Circulation in South and West

State	Bank Circulation [a] (April 4, 1832)	Total Circulation [b] (1834 or 1835) of state banks)	Per cent of Total
Virginia	$1,091,095	$5,598,392	20
North Carolina	887,685	958,934	93
South Carolina	1,003,665	2,156,318 [c]	50 [d]
Georgia	1,317,060	3,694,329 [c]	35
Alabama	1,276,315	2,054,471	52
Louisiana	3,566,560	5,114,082	70
Mississippi	794,130	1,510,426	53
Missouri	395,675	. . . [c]	
Tennessee	1,609,885	1,520,880	106
Kentucky	1,994,955	87,564	
Ohio	1,128,460	5,221,520 [c]	21
Illinois	No branch	No State Bank [e]	
Indiana	No branch	. . . [f]	

[a] *Senate Documents,* 23rd Congress, 2nd Session, vol. 11, doc. 17.
[b] John J. Knox, *A History of Banking in the United States* (New York: B. Rhodes and Co., 1900), pp. 522–793.
[c] Figure given is for 1835. All other figures are for 1834.
[d] Total for this state is marked "incomplete."
[e] Even as late as 1835 the circulation of two state banks recently chartered was only $178,810.
[f] Only one bank existed, and it was winding up its affairs. The State Bank of Indiana was chartered in 1834.

Those states offering petitions from two-thirds to all of their state banks were the very ones with the highest ratio of United States Bank notes to state bank notes, i.e., North Carolina, Alabama, Louisiana, and Mississippi. Those states offering the fewest petitions, or none at all, from state banks for renewal were those with the lowest ratio—except for Ohio, which gave strong support. Ohio's ratio of note circulation was 1 to 5. Smith's findings supported the memorials. In 1822, 73 per cent of all the

Bank's notes were issued in the South and West. In 1827, 71 per cent were issued there. Between 1822 and 1827 personal loans increased for the Bank as a whole. In 1822 about 75 per cent of them were made in the South and West. In 1827 about 60 per cent were made there.[4] In 1828 notes in circulation rose by 1.3 million dollars and most of these were in the South and West.[5]

That New Orleans was not exaggerating its position with respect to bills of exchange can be seen from the following table:

Totals—Discounts and Exchange of the Bank in Three Areas [a]

July, 1831

New York Branch	$ 4,370,000
Philadelphia	8,789,000
New Orleans Branch	10,282,000

July, 1832

New York Branch	5,597,000
Philadelphia	7,963,000
New Orleans Branch	12,911,000

[a] Ralph C. H. Catterall, *The Second Bank of the United States* (Chicago: University of Chicago Press, 1903), p. 398.

The charge of hostility caused by greed and jealousy of the United States Bank as a competitor of the state banks is refuted by the Commercial Bank of Cincinnati. Although there is the recognition of the Bank as a competitor, the general good of the community will be greatly reduced if the Bank charter is not renewed. The memorial goes so far as to view the competition between state banks and the Bank of the United States as mutually beneficial and healthy, keeping the Bank from becoming a monopoly and checking excess issues of state bank notes. Govan's contrast of the relationship between the Bank and the

[4] Walter B. Smith, *Economic Aspects of the Second Bank of the United States* (Cambridge: Harvard University Press, 1953), p. 241.
[5] *Ibid.*, p. 235.

state banks under Cheves and under Biddle lends credence to
the memorials. Under the former they had been mutually antagonistic. Neither was able to perform its proper function. But
under Biddle's policies they became collaborators in providing
credit facilities for an expanding economy. The local banks supplied local needs and the Bank supplied the means for the internal exchanges of products throughout the country.[6] This
capacity to appreciate the long-run general good over the bank's
own short-run particular good is made clear in the memorial
from the two North Carolina Banks.

The memorialists state that they have had extensive dealings
with the United States Bank in areas almost certain to bring conflict. Because of the upright and liberal treatment by the Bank,
such conflict did not occur. It may be, say the memorialists, that
banks of North Carolina would have a wider field for profitable
operations if the Bank did not exist, but such possible benefits
cannot compare with those derived from the Bank's equalizing
of exchanges, its maintaining a sound currency, and promoting habits of punctuality and good faith. Nothing has so pow-
erfully produced these effects in North Carolina as the in-
direct but salutary control of local issues by the United States
Bank.[7]

The liberal treatment of the state banks in the South and West
by the Bank is reflected in a sample check on the item in the
Bank's records called "due from state banks." In 1822 about 66
per cent of the balances due were from banks in the South and
West. In 1826, 100 per cent of the balances were from there and
in 1827, 50 per cent.[8] In the foreign exchange market, the Bank
was the leading dealer in foreign exchange in the United States
and equalized exchanges. It drew on its balances and also bor-
rowed (abroad) and drew when rates were high. When rates

---

[6] Thomas Payne Govan, *Nicholas Biddle, Nationalist and Public Banker,
1786–1844* (Chicago: University of Chicago Press, 1959), p. 86.
[7] *Executive Documents*, 22nd Congress, 1st Session, vol. IV, doc. 166.
[8] Smith, p. 241.

were low, it bought bills and accumulated foreign balances. The Bank was also the most important dealer in domestic bills, buying in the West and selling in the East.[9] When foreign exchange was in short supply, the Bank would intervene so as to prevent the rate from remaining long beyond the point where large shipments of specie were required.[10]

When it is remembered that the two banks of North Carolina, representing two-thirds of the state banks in that state, did not follow solid conservative so-called "good banking" practices but rather were constantly overextended and in danger of failure, it is hard to accept the theory that the restraining hand of the United States Bank was deeply offensive, especially to the banks in the South and Southwest where banking practices were most open to question. The North Carolina banks were archetypes of "loose" banking principles:

In 1825 the state banks of North Carolina, old and hardened offenders, which had refused specie payments at pleasure since 1822, were taken in hand, but after ten months' struggle the attempt was given up because it was impossible to continue it "without a further supply" of branch notes. It was only in 1827 that this deficiency was made good by the invention of branch drafts, which at last gave the bank the means of securing control by the process of exchanging branch notes for state-bank notes. As a consequence the North Carolina state banks yielded in 1828, making an agreement with the Bank of the United States to pay specie and settle their balances regularly. . . . Thus in 1830 McDuffie expressed the belief that North Carolina notes were the only ones at a discount, and these were depreciated only 1 or 2 per cent, while a year earlier they had been at 5 to 8 and 12 to 14 per cent. Even Gouge admits that the Bank of the United States had succeeded in North Carolina.[11]

Similarly, the Planters' Bank of Mississippi in its memorial stresses the benefits of sound currency. The Bank of the State of

[9] *Ibid.*, pp. 241–43.   [10] Govan, p. 87.
    [11] Catterall, pp. 441–42 quoting Niles Register, Vol. XXIII, XXIV, and XXXIV. Also Huske to Biddle, July 29, 1826, NBP and Biddle to Huske, April 17, 1828, PLB. Also H.R. 358, 21st Congress, 1st Session, p. 18, April 13, 1830, and Gouge (Cobbett's edition), p. 162.

Mississippi mentions with pleasure the salutary effect of the Bank on the state banks.[12] These two banks constituted the total of all state banks in Mississippi at the time.

Perhaps when historians stress the restraining and controlling hand of the Bank as a cause of state bank hostility they overlook the fact that this restraint and control was reciprocal. If, through overextension of its loans the Bank fell in debt to the state banks, it lost its position of dominance, and, as Catterall said,[13] under these circumstances there was the added risk of the Bank's creating a pressure so intense as to lead to its own bankruptcy. The Bank of Cincinnati makes mention of this reciprocal function. It would appear that the state banks were more aware of it than later writers have recognized.

Let us turn now to pro-Bank memorials from citizens—of which, according to Congressional records, there appear to have been about 118 presented. Of these 118, 44 came from the South and West. There were 16 from Ohio, 16 from Kentucky, 6 from Indiana, 2 from Tennessee, 2 from Alabama, 1 from Virginia, and 1 from South Carolina. It is hard for us to do anything from a quantitative point of view because very few of these memorials state how many signatures are affixed to them. However, the contents of some and the identities of the senders, when mentioned, prove of interest. For example, the only favorable one sent from South Carolina came from the state chamber of commerce. Several from Pennsylvania were sent by persons calling themselves "traders with the West." Many memorials came from "merchants and mechanics."

To gain some idea of the economic reasons for support of the Bank in those states where state banks did not exist, let us first

---

[12] A copy of both memorials is included in NBP, February 23, 1832.

[13] The state banks and the branches of the Bank settled their balances with each other periodically. The Bank by discounting less and issuing fewer notes than the state banks held more state bank notes than the state banks held of United States Bank notes. Consequently, specie could be required of the state banks in settlement of the difference owed the Bank. If the United States Bank extended its notes beyond that of the state banks, the situation was reversed and the state banks could demand specie payment of the Bank. Catterall, pp. 436–39.

look at a petition for renewal from the citizens of Bracken County, Kentucky.[14]

In their opinion, the question of the constitutionality of the Bank has long been settled. Moreover, the return of prosperity in the Union generally, but particularly in the western section, has been contemporaneous with the creation of the Bank and commensurate with the gradual success of the institution. Everything connected with commerce, agriculture, and manufacturing in the Valley of the Mississippi has assumed a fixed and stable character in proportion as the Bank itself has become firm and capable of shedding among the people a well-dispensed moderate capital through their well-managed branches.

The Atlantic seaports, from the long accumulation of capital and wealth, and from the firm establishment of state banks of their own, may not so immediately perceive the beneficial effects of the Bank. But for them (the memorialists of Kentucky), just emerging from the first phase of settlement and just throwing off the character of clearers of the land, the influence of this Bank, affording as it does a large part of their capital, is interwoven with their very commercial and trading existence. This fact is acknowledged, they assert, by every grade of citizen from laborer to capitalist.

This memorial is especially interesting since it lends credence to the suggestion made earlier in analyzing the distribution of votes cast on matters pertaining to the Bank. It was there discovered that the far western areas of both the nation and of New York state, contrary to most theories, supported the Bank. Here the petitioners describe themselves as just emerging from a frontier state of development and urge that because of this the Bank is more essential to them than to the more developed areas of the country. In the previous chapter it was noted that the only state bank in Virginia, of the four in existence, to send a memorial

---

[14] *Executive Documents*, 22nd Congress, 1st Session, vol. IV, doc. 165.

was the one located in the western part of the state—the part which later became West Virginia. This, again, is another fact supporting the theory that the western or newer areas were pro-Bank areas.

The other noteworthy item in the memorial is the recognition that agriculture, commerce, and manufacturing all develop *together* as the Bank develops and that every citizen from laborer to capitalist is aware of this relation. This suggests that we perhaps do violence to the actual situation in the West when we try to single out a group such as the "poor western farmers" as ringleaders in destroying the Bank.

The citizens of Louisville, Kentucky, declare in their memorial that the states of Kentucky, Indiana, Illinios, Missouri, and Tennessee have no banking institutions of their own. Ohio and Alabama have none of extended credit. Therefore the whole of the West is dependent on the Bank, for it provides the *only* circulating medium. If the charter of the Bank is not renewed, farmers, merchants, and manufacturers alike will suffer fearfully.[15]

There were eleven separate memorials signed by "Citizens of Kentucky." These state that Kentucky is entirely dependent on the United States Bank for exchange and discounts. If the renewal of the Bank's charter fails, ruin will be brought on the public works of internal improvement along with all else.[16]

Included in the Biddle Manuscripts is a printed copy of another memorial that circulated through many counties.[17] It asserts that the Bank preserves sound currency, encourages agriculture, commerce, and manufacturing. If its charter is not renewed, this will devalue property and check internal improvements thereby throwing thousands of citizens out of work. It will paralyze industry and destroy confidence. The citizens of

[15] *Executive Documents,* 22nd Congress, 1st Session, vol. IV, doc. 142.
[16] *Executive Documents,* 22nd Congress, 1st Session, vol. IV, doc. 111.
[17] NBP, January 28, 1832.

Kentucky are entirely dependent on the Bank for exchange and discounts.

Throughout these memorials there is again a noticeable absence of a distinction between the interests of the farmer with respect to the Bank on the one hand, and those of commerce or manufacturing on the other—a distinction which some historians have had an undue tendency to draw.

It might be objected that one ought not argue for western support of the Bank from the contents of these memorials, in view of the bias inherent in their having been written by friends of the Bank. That is, while they might *identify* the economic reasons for supporting the Bank in the West, they tell us nothing about the *extent* of such support in that area. It does seem significant, however, that no state bank memorials and only three citizens' memorials were sent to Congress from the South and West combined asking that the Bank's charter not be renewed. These three memorials came from the 10th Congressional District of Ohio,[18] from Hamilton County, Indiana,[19] and from South Carolina.[20] Each of the latter two also sent a pro-Bank memorial.[21]

Several branch Bank officers, when asked by Biddle to get memorials from friends of the Bank, answered that they dared not do so for fear of setting off counter-memorials. Presumably if they kept quiet so would the Bank's opponents. Hence, circulating a pro-Bank memorial should have been the signal for the opposition to begin. Yet in the whole West and South with a total of 44 citizens' memorials and about 15 state bank memorials in favor of the Bank forwarded to Congress, only 3 anti-Bank citizens' memorials were produced. Moreover, as will be seen from correspondence referred to in subsequent chapters, the anti-Bank forces in Washington were attempting to institute coun-

[18] *House Journal*, 22nd Congress, 1st Session, p. 474.
[19] *Senate Journal*, 22nd Congress, 1st Session, p. 197.
[20] *Executive Documents*, 22nd Congress, 1st Session, vol. VI, doc. 237.
[21] *Senate Journal*, 22nd Congress, 1st Session, p. 215.

termeasures. If the state banks and the populace of this area were as hostile to the Bank as historians have claimed, one would think they might have mustered more than three memorials.

There is another indicator of pro-Bank feeling to be found from examining the areas [22] requesting that branches of the Bank be established in their vicinity. Between 1826 and 1832 there were 74 requests for branches, 66 of which were refused.[23] Of the 74, five came from territories of the United States; four from Florida and one from Michigan. Of the remaining 69, 48 came from the South and West. There were requests from Virginia that branches be established in four places there. Once again these places were in the western part of the state—Wheeling, Petersburg, and Danville, located in what is now West Virginia, and Abingdon. North Carolina requested six branches to be scattered throughout the state: Washington in the northeast, Charlotte in the west, Milton in the north central, Raleigh in the central, Newbern and Tarborough in the east central, and Wilmington in the southeast. South Carolina requested only two, Columbia in the center of the state and Cheraw in the northeast. Georgia requested four, also scattered throughout the state: Augusta in the east central, Macon in the center, Clarksville in the northeast, and Columbus in the west central. Lastly, Alabama asked for seven, which were refused. Florence, Athens, Courtland, Huntsville,[24] and Tuscumbia are all in the northern part of the state on the Tennessee River, which flows into the Mississippi. Montgomery, in the center of Alabama, is situated on the Alabama River running to Mobile. The last place, Colossus, is no longer shown on the map of that state. A branch at Mobile was asked for and established in 1826.

[22] Often groups of citizens requested a branch. Sometimes the state legislature would make the request or the governor of the state would write Biddle for one.

[23] Senate Documents, 23rd Congress, 2nd Session vol. II.

[24] Not listed in Senate Documents of the 23rd Congress, 2nd Session but appears in a letter from Biddle to Smith, February 15, 1831, PLB.

In the Southwest, Mississippi and Louisiana made no requests that were refused. Mississippi asked for and received a branch at Natchez in 1830.

In the West, Ohio led with seven requests. Five areas, Zanesville, Dayton, Chillicothe, Circleville, and Portland are all in the southern part of the state. Cleveland is in the north on Lake Erie. All six areas are located on water and the five southern ones are on rivers all running into the Ohio. Only Columbus is not so situated. But a letter from John McLean [25] to Biddle dated July 13, 1831, explains this. McLean wrote that several of his friends, since he arrived in Columbus, have expressed anxiety to know whether their request for a branch will be agreed to. This town is the seat of the state government, and although its business at present might not be quite as great as in some other parts of the state, it will shortly be much greater when the canal is finished. There is good grazing land all around Columbus, and many sales of cattle are made to drovers, who depend upon bank accommodation to make their payments. Since these drovers are preferred by banks and individuals with money to lend,[26] a branch established at Columbus will be certain to have a large amount of business.

Indiana requested six branches, one listed but not named. The others are somewhat scattered: Madison in the southeast, Vincennes in the southwest, Lafayette in the northwest, Terre Haute in the midwest, and Indianapolis in the center. Kentucky asked for a branch at Frankfort, quite near the already existing branch in Lexington in the northern part of the state, and one at Hopkinsville in the southwest. Kentucky already had two branches of the Bank, the other being at Louisville. Missouri asked for and was given one at St. Louis in 1829. Finally, Tennessee requested four—Knoxville, Jackson, and Memphis, all in the south, and Clarksville in the west. In addition she was given a

[25] Representative from Kentucky and Postmaster General under Adams and Jackson.
[26] McLean to Biddle, July 13, 1831, NBP.

branch in Nashville. Clearly these requests bespeak a real need for the Bank in contrast to the rest of the country excluding territories, which totally asked for only 21, of which 17 were not granted. The bulk of the 48 requests of the South and West poured in between the years 1830 and 1832.

Another source of support might be the state legislatures. The Louisiana state legislature instructed the Senate and requested the House of Representatives in Washington to vote for the renewal of the charter.[27] It will be recalled that Louisiana obeyed instructions and voted 100 per cent in favor of the Bank.[28] Mississippi in 1828 had legislated against permitting a branch of the Bank in Mississippi,[29] but by 1830 had changed its position. In that year the law was repealed and the legislature forwarded to Congress a petition for a branch at Natchez. From this action one might infer that the state legislature was generally pro-Bank. There is even some indication that the people of Mississippi preferred a branch of the Bank to a new state bank. We find Biddle writing to Stephen Duncan of Natchez that he is glad the proposed state bank is discouraged by "the sober people of Mississippi." He feels Duncan's bank and the branch will serve adequately the state's needs.[30]

Alabama's legislature can also be classified as more or less pro-Bank. James Jackson of Florence, Alabama, wrote Biddle on January 29, 1832, that a large majority of the state legislature has rejected a resolution against rechartering the Bank. After this a bill was proposed that would forbid the establishment of a branch in Alabama without the consent of the legislature. This also failed. Were it not for the effect of the President's opinions, particularly on the demagogues, Jackson claims, Alabama would most decidedly be in favor of rechartering.[31]

[27] *House Journal,* 22nd Congress, 1st Session.
[28] See the Louisiana vote, Chapter II, p. 9.
[29] Biddle to Jaudon, August 4, 1830, PLB.
[30] Biddle to Duncan, August 5, 1830, PLB.
[31] Jackson to Biddle, January 29, 1832, NBP. We know that by 1833 the Alabama state legislature was inquiring into the expediency of begging Con-

One branch of Georgia's legislature also favored the Bank. In a letter to Richard Wilde, a member of the House of Representatives from Georgia, Biddle wrote that he is glad to learn that the anti-Bank resolution in the Georgia legislature failed by a decisive vote.[32] Though not specifically mentioning the legislature, Charles Jared Ingersoll [33] wrote Biddle from Washington on February 2, 1832, that a majority of North Carolina members of Congress will vote pro-Bank. He went on to say that the sentiment throughout the state was so strong that any member from North Carolina voting against the Bank endangered his own reelection.[34] Benjamin O'Fallon, president of the branch Bank in Missouri, wrote Biddle on February 6, 1832, that the Senate of Indiana has passed a resolution instructing their senators in Washington to vote in favor of the Bank. He says it also will pass the House by a large majority.[35] Herman Cope of Cincinnati wrote that a memorial has been sent to the state legislature in Ohio to petition Congress for renewal.[36] In January, 1826, the Ohio legislature repealed its enactment outlawing a branch of the Bank.[37]

That the Missouri state legislature favored the Bank is highly doubtful. This was the home state of Thomas Benton whose hard money beliefs and anti-Bank attitudes were well known.

---

gress to recharter the Bank. See Thomas H. Clark, *Memorial Record of Alabama* (2 vols., Madison: Brant and Fuller, 1893), vol. I.

[32] Biddle to Wilde, January 6, 1832, PLB. Also Niles' *Register* of January 21, 1832, states that a report and resolutions against rechartering the Bank passed the Senate in Georgia on December 22, 1831, but were *laid on the table* for the remainder of the session in the House.

[33] A close friend of Nicholas Biddle's and a member of the House of Representatives from Philadelphia.

[34] Ingersoll to Biddle, February 2, 1832, NBP.

[35] O'Fallon to Biddle, February 6, 1832, NBP. Whether or not the House passed this resolution cannot be verified in the *House Journal* of Indiana because the *Journal* ends February 3, 1832. There is a record, however, in the *Laws of the State of Indiana*, p. 288, that a joint resolution was passed by the State General Assembly requesting the president and directors of the Bank to locate one or more branches of the Bank in the state of Indiana.

[36] Cope to Biddle, February 4, 1832, NBP.

[37] Eugene H. Roseboom and Francis P. Weisenburger, *A history of Ohio* (Columbus: Ohio State Archaeological Society, 1953), p. 87.

He was the foremost leader in the Senate in the attack on the Bank. Benjamin O'Fallon, in the letter just mentioned, wrote that of all the western states Missouri will give the greatest opposition because of the extreme ignorance of the majority in banking matters. Newspapers seldom reached them, and those that did were under Benton's thumb.[38] Action by the state legislature was taken after Jackson's reelection. It was resolved by the Senate in November of 1832 [39] and the General Assembly in December of 1832 [40] that they approved of the veto message of President Jackson on the grounds that the Bank was unconstitutional and a monopoly. Further, the General Assembly instructed Missouri's United States senators and requested their members in the United States House of Representatives to vote against any bill brought before Congress for the purpose of rechartering the Bank.

As to Kentucky, the Jackson party passed resolutions in 1831 advocating a modified charter. Col. H. M. Johnson presided. He was thought to be hostile to the Bank but Verplanck [41] said he was not.[42]

Some of the southern and western state legislatures were not in session between January 16, 1832, and July 10, 1832, the date of the veto. Considering this limitation, we may say that a sizable number of state legislatures in the South and West gave good indications of pro-Bank feeling. However, there is one state, Virginia, where there is positive evidence of hostility. Earlier it was shown that Nicholas Biddle looked for little support from this state. In addition there are several interesting letters from R. Robertson, of the Richmond branch, about the situation

---

[38] For an account of the changing attitudes of the newspapers toward the Bank and Benton see William Nisbet Chambers, *Old Bullion Benton* (Boston: Little, Brown, 1956), pp. 168–70, 187, 188.

[39] *Missouri Statutes and Laws*, 7, 1832.

[40] *Laws of the State of Missouri passed at the First Session of the Seventh General Assembly*, p. 61.

[41] Representative from New York, a Jacksonian but an advocate of the Bank.

[42] Webb to Biddle, February 6, 1832, NBP.

in Virginia.[43] Robertson wrote that his congressional district, through the efforts of its representative in Washington, is against the Bank. Nowhere are people as inveterately hostile to the Bank as there in Virginia, and this is the result of corporate interests, personal enmity, and blind political devotion to the views of the Secretary of State.[44] People everywhere in the country are in favor of the Bank, but the Jacksonians appear determined to make it a political issue.[45]

It is apparent from these letters that, just as in Georgia where there was overt hostility among the state banks, so in Virginia some groups definitely opposed the Bank. Yet such cases seem to have been the exception. Judging from citizens' and state bank memorials, the numerous requests for branches, the state legislatures' actions with respect to the Bank, and the voting patterns in Congress, we have found the evidence of friendliness toward the Bank sufficiently strong to warrant asking how the contrary theory should have gained such prominence.

Originally, when the Bank began with William Jones as president, the notes of the Bank were freely and indiscriminately issued. The course of exchange was usually against the South and West, and the branches of the Bank in these areas issued as many notes as they wished. As a consequence the Bank's capital was drawn to the South and West. To end this state of affairs, in August, 1818, each branch was prohibited from redeeming any United States branch notes except its own.[46] Essentially this left the country with no common medium of exchange. At the same time the note issues were restricted by $3,000,000. At this point Jones retired, and Langdon Cheves of South Carolina took over

---

[43] For the moment only the letters written March 12, and 23, 1831, will be discussed. The other correspondence will be examined after New England and the Middle states have been analyzed.

[44] Robertson to Biddle, March 12, 1831, NBP.

[45] Robertson to Biddle, March 23, 1831, NBP.

[46] I.e., each branch issued its own notes and redeemed only its own after August, 1818.

the direction of the Bank's affairs. His policy was to continue the contraction. The Western offices were denied the right to issue any notes, and the circulation dropped to almost nothing in this section.

In 1823 Nicholas Biddle became president and had very different ideas as to the circulation of the Bank's notes. He was especially anxious that relief be brought to the South and West. The branches were again permitted to issue their notes up to a specified amount. These notes would move to the Atlantic offices of the Bank for redemption in specie because the exchanges were against the West and South. Western and southern debtor balances were sent to the East in branch bank notes issued by branches in the South and West. To offset this drain Biddle encouraged the southern and western branches to buy inland bills of exchange. When these bills were paid on presentation in the East, they provided the funds out of which the bank notes could be paid. By 1831 the note circulation was double that of 1826. It was not, therefore, until 1831 that the Bank became truly national and fulfilled the purposes for which it was originally intended.[47]

The West and South, then, had had rather a hard time of it during the early history of the Bank, and substantial benefit could not be felt until about 1828. It was in 1830, it will be recalled, that the southern and western requests for branches were received in such abundance.

Several of the letters reflect this changing attitude. Herman Cope of the branch in Cincinnati wrote Biddle that both of the two public papers in that city formerly were opposed but now are friendly.[48] Hunter at an agency of the Bank in Macon, Georgia, wrote that people of that state are becoming more favorable to the Bank.[49] James Jackson of Alabama mentions that

---

[47] Catterall, pp. 404–07. [48] Cope to Biddle, February 4, 1832, NBP.
[49] Hunter to Biddle, April 23, 1831, NBP.

the behavior of the legislature shows the change of opinion there.[50] A marked change of opinion had occurred in Ohio.[51] Even Missouri developed a sizable pro-Bank group which was strong enough to elect to Congress Representative Ashley, a Bank supporter, who ran against Wells, a pro-Benton candidate.[52]

There had been, then, considerable hostility in the South and West at an earlier period than is being considered here. When it is remembered that following the veto severe contraction took place again which once more hurt the South and West most, it is not to be wondered why hostility has been ascribed to this part of the country. No doubt at both periods strong hostility did exist. But for the crucial period between 1828 and 1832, when the benefits of Biddle's policies were being truly felt by the people, favorable attitudes have been overlooked. As a result it has been thought necessary to develop theories to explain why these areas of the country were not ready yet for a national bank—the discipline of which was supposedly out of step with their tendencies to expand.

On the contrary, from the evidence presented it appears that when the Bank actually fulfilled the purposes for which it was intended, it was much appreciated. But, as would be most natural, it was resented when it acted otherwise and hurt the economic interests of this part of the country.

Now, Catterall's book was the most significant work devoted exclusively to the Bank. It was published in 1903 prior to the panic of 1907 and the subsequent legislation establishing the Federal Reserve Banks. Accustomed to a system of national banks, his historical perspective was not that of today's historians who are conditioned to the benefits derived from the Federal Reserve.[53] Consequently, Catterall was not asking the same

[50] Jackson to Biddle, January 29, 1832, NBP.
[51] Roseboom and Weisenburger, p. 87.   [52] Chambers, pp. 186, 187.
[53] Bray Hammond wrote *Banks and Politics* because Catterall did not appreciate the role of the Bank as a central bank.

historical question, i.e., he was not specifically investigating the attitudes of state banks or the populace to the Bank after it functioned more as a central bank functions. Rather, he was taking a long look at the full twenty years of the Bank's history to determine its opponents. For most of those twenty years the South and West were in fact hostile. Add to this his faulty analysis of the 1832 vote which led to the same generalization, and it is not strange that Catterall attributed to the state banks and to the people of this area in general a determined opposition.

Actually there is little that needs explanation. These people were very short of capital and lacked a currency. For the most part they bought and sold through New Orleans and needed a ready and stable market for their bills of exchange. Only the Second United States Bank with its system of branches, together with Biddle's mature policy, could fulfill this need. When the two combined, the Bank's economic benefits were recognized and enjoyed.

6

New England

TURNING NOW to the traditionally Federalist-Whig, pro-Bank area, New England, one expects to find there the firmest and most enthusiastic support of the Second United States Bank to be met with in any part of the country.

Biddle wrote to Joseph Wingate, Jr., president of the Portland, Maine, branch of the Bank on January 16, 1832, suggesting for Wingate's consideration whether the citizens or state banks could be induced to petition for the renewal of the charter.[1] On January 23rd Wingate replied that the friends of the Bank are saying they should not send a memorial for fear the Bank's enemies will get up a counter-memorial. The political situation in Maine is too pro-Jackson.[2] Here was a case, just as in South Carolina, of hostility being sufficiently strong to keep the friends of the Bank from forwarding any memorials because of the likelihood of their opponents doing the same. All that came from Maine was a petition from the state legislature instructing its senators and requesting its representatives in Washington not to vote for the renewal of the Bank's charter.[3] However, Senator Holmes of Maine thought those who instructed him needed instruction themselves. He believed the instructions they sent him originally were sent to Maine from Washington then back to him in Washington.[4] There were no memorials either from state banks or from citizens' groups.

Supporting Wingate's statement of the pro-administration sentiment in Maine is the fact that this state gave Jackson 33,984

[1] Biddle to Wingate, January 16, 1832, PLB.
[2] Wingate to Biddle, January 23, 1832, NBP.
[3] *Executive Documents*, 22nd Congress, 1st Session, vol. IV, doc. 169.
[4] Niles' *Register*, March 31, 1832.

votes, Clay 27,362, and Wirt 841 votes in the 1832 election.[5] The attitude of the state banks as such cannot be determined. All that can be said is that they failed to rally to active support of the Bank.

From Portsmouth, New Hampshire, Jeremiah Mason,[6] president of the branch located there, answered Biddle's request for help by writing that there is no problem about getting up a memorial, but, as soon as he does, the Jacksonians will make a countermove:

The administration party is thoroughly organized for action as its leaders may direct. The opposition has no efficient organization. With *equal pains* we might obtain a divided majority, in property and respectability, but we should be beat in numbers. The superiority in the character of our memorialists could not be easily shown in Congress. I do not, therefore, deem it expedient to attempt to procure memorials from our citizens at large.

Of our Banks I have better hopes. I have seen the Presidents and some of the most influential Directors of four of the six Banks in this town. They are favorably disposed and will move willingly, in case the Boston Banks give the lead, and I think they will do it without that ——.[7] I shall write to Boston and ascertain what is doing there. The other two Banks are under adverse influence. One will remain silent. The other will go against us, if requested to do so from Washington.

The numerous Country Banks in this state with the exception of two only, I evaluate to be favorably disposed. I am well acquainted with the most influential directors, and will write to them. I depend with confidence on their cooperation, in case the Massachusetts Banks shall be seen moving in the same course. . . .

The letter goes on to state that the reason the Massachusetts banks must take the lead is because of the timidity of the New Hampshire banks.[8]

---

[5] Samuel Rhea Gammon, *Presidential Campaign of 1832* (Baltimore: Johns Hopkins Press, 1922), p. 170.

[6] The most talented lawyer of the times in Webster's opinion. See Claude Moore Fuess, *Daniel Webster* (2 vols., Boston: Little, Brown & Co., 1930), I, 108, footnote 1.

[7] The last word in this sentence is illegible in the manuscript.

[8] Mason to Biddle, January 23, 1832, NBP.

This letter points up two things of importance. First, the state banks of New Hampshire in the main were not hostile to the Bank. Second, the few that were against the Bank appear to have been motivated by political reasons, rather than because of having been restrained by or in competition with the Bank.

Actually recorded as having been presented to Congress were ten state bank memorials from the Bank of New Hampshire in Exeter, the Union Bank in Portsmouth, the Farmers' Bank of Amherst, another Bank of New Hampshire, the Bank of Rockingham in Portsmouth, the Bank of Lebanon, the Bank of Winnepesaukee, the Bank of Piscataque, the Bank of Stratford in Dover, and the Bank of Dover.[9] According to Knox[10] there were twenty-one state banks in 1831. Ten memorials, then, seem to have represented a healthy proportion of support. In addition, two citizens' memorials were sent from Charleston and Lebanon; both places are situated on the Connecticut River.[11]

Just after Biddle forwarded to Congress the Bank's request for renewal of its charter, he wrote to Jeremiah Mason telling him of the Bank's action and explaining why the action has been taken at this time. Biddle remarks that he has put down the whole of the New Hampshire delegation as enemies of the Bank and asks Mason whether their erroneous views might not be explained to them.[12]

Keeping in mind that New Hampshire gave Jackson 25,146 votes in the 1832 election and Clay 19,454, with none for Wirt,[13] and recalling that New Hampshire's Congressmen voted 86 per cent against the Bank, one is struck again by the inappropriateness of Catterall's analysis of New England. With respect to that section he asserted that all the senators voted in favor of the Bank except Hill of New Hampshire, the implica-

[9] *House Journal*, 22nd Congress, 1st Session, pp. 286, 293, 330, 385, 413, 444.
[10] John J. Knox, *A History of Banking in the United States* (New York: B. Rhodes & Co., 1900), p. 338.
[11] *House Journal*, 22nd Congress, 1st Session, pp. 413, 444.
[12] Biddle to Mason, January 7, 1832, PLB.   [13] Gammon, p. 170.

tion being that New England could be disposed of as altogether pro-Bank. Both Maine and New Hampshire, as we have seen, were decidedly against the Bank and had made their position sufficiently well felt so as to limit the action of the Bank's supporters, who appear to have been in the minority. And if we may assume from the letters of Mason and Wingate that the Bank issue in this part of the country seems to have been a matter of politics, then from the election returns we are forced to conclude that the Bank's supporters *were* a minority in both states.

Printed in full in the Executive Documents is the memorial of the Farmers' Bank of Amherst, New Hampshire.[14] It contains arguments that are especially interesting.

First, it denies that the Bank is hostile to state banks. If there were no Bank, many more state banks would come into existence, and this would offer more competition to the state banks' operations than that coming from the Bank. The state banks, presently increasing in numbers, realize as high a profit as the legislatures ought to sanction.

State banks, being local in their sphere of influence, bring no new capital into their respective states. They simply employ the capital already there; capital which would be employed—although not so conveniently—without a Bank charter.

The state banks' capacity to ward off a recession is limited—the banks move down with the downward swing of the cycle. But the Bank can take funds from one part of the country where they are not needed and bring them to a part where they are. For example, a recent oversupply of capital in Boston had caused a drop in the interest rate to 4½ per cent. The Bank thereupon took action and transferred capital to places where it was scarce. Moreover, if the entire country were facing a recession, the Bank might borrow abroad and bring relief everywhere.

[14] *Executive Documents*, 22nd Congress, 1st Session, vol. IV, doc. 110.

The memorial goes on to recommend that the new charter should require the Bank to pay a bonus of 1 or 1½ per cent on its capital—which should amount to $50,000,000—to the Treasury. This might go either to the states in which branches are located, or wholly to the United States. Probably the latter would be preferable; it could go to defray the expenses of government, reduce import duties, or promote internal improvements.

Prophetically, the memorial closes with the assertion that if the Bank is not rechartered none ever will be.

The first argument in the memorial is one rarely, if ever, alluded to in the literature on the Bank: that the state banks might prefer the competition of the United States Bank to the additional competition arising from the state banks which would spring into existence at the demise of the Second Bank. The customary view has been just the opposite—that the Bank's role as competitor was the cause of state bank hostility.

Second, that the Bank acted so as to "lean against the prevailing wind" has been emphasized often by historians, but that this was understood and appreciated by state banks has been seldom suggested. The same holds true of the Bank's capacity to borrow from abroad and thus bring country-wide relief were the whole nation involved at the same time in a recession, at which time there would be no surplus capital in one part of the country to transfer to another.

The other economic argument supporting renewal of the Bank's charter—that local banks introduce no new capital into their respective states whereas the Bank does—has been noted in other state bank memorials from the South and West.

At the time Nicholas Biddle was writing to the presidents and cashiers of the various branches of the Bank enlisting their efforts in support of the Bank, Heman Allen, a Vermont member of the House of Representatives in Congress happened to be at home in Burlington, Vermont, perhaps from illness, instead of attending the legislative session in Washington. Biddle thus chose to correspond with him rather than with the president or cashier of the branch bank in Burlington, and wrote on January 16th requesting citizens' and state bank memorials.[15]

Allen promptly responded. On January 29th he forwarded a memorial from the Banks and citizens of Burlington and St. Albans. At the same time he included memorials from the Bank of Vergennes, and from the citizens of Plattsburg in the state of New York. He wrote that more memorials are in progress and will be forwarded. He further advises Biddle that any senator or representative will present these documents to their respective house in Washington.[16]

On the same day Allen sent another letter mentioning memorials he has sent from the citizens of Plattsburg, Madisonville, and Port Kent in the state of New York.[17] He points out that there is no party feeling in these memorials. He enclosed more memorials; there was one from the Bank of Montpelier, one from the Supreme Court of the state, and one from the citizens of Middlebury (the court was in session there); enclosed also were memorials from the towns of Williston and Highgate. In the memorial from Middlebury is the name Ira Stewart, a director of the Bank of Rutland. But Allen expects a direct expression to arrive from that Bank and from the citizens there.

He enclosed three newspapers of the opposite political view. The Jackson paper of Middlebury wrote in *favor of the Bank*. The letter advises as to which members of Congress should present each memorial. Allen concludes that before going further, he will await word from Biddle.[18]

On February 18th Allen wrote again, enclosing the promised memorial from the Bank of Rutland. He predicts that the Banks of Danville, Chelsea, Windsor, Brattleboro, and Bennington will

[15] Biddle to Allen, January 16, 1832, PLB.
[16] Allen to Biddle, January 29, 1832, NBP.
[17] Located in Essex County, New York, on Lake Champlain, not far from Burlington on the opposite or western side of the lake.
[18] Allen to Biddle, January 29, 1832, NBP.

do likewise,[19] and another letter on the same day enclosed memorials from Danville and Montpelier.[20]

Horatio Seymour [21] wrote Biddle from Washington at this time telling him of the presentation of the Vermont memorials. He informs Biddle that all the Vermont delegation is pro-Bank but will want some modifications to the charter. First, they desire that no branches be established in a state without the consent of the state, and second, that the Bank be taxed on its capital at the same rate the state banks are taxed.[22]

Finally, on February 27th Biddle wrote Allen, still in Burlington, that he fears the friends of the Bank will join with its enemies because they are afraid that agitation of the Bank question now will injure Jackson's chances in the coming election.[23]

The foregoing correspondence reflects several things of importance. First, it reveals the broad support that existed in Vermont for the Bank. The national representatives, the citizens, and the state banks showed considerable unanimity. It should be mentioned that even the state legislature forwarded instructions to Congress to vote in favor of rechartering the Bank.[24] Knox reported ten state banks in existence in Vermont in 1827.[25] The congressional records show that seven state bank petitions were presented and memorials from the citizens of twelve towns,[26] not counting the one from the Bank of Montpelier, which means that eight of the ten state banks supported the Bank.

The correspondence also indicates how Bank support originally crossed party lines. The memorials from citizens in New York show no party feeling; i.e., they were signed by members

[19] Allen to Biddle, February 18, 1832, NBP.   [20] Ibid.
[21] Senator from Vermont.
[22] Seymour to Biddle, January 29, 1832, NBP. These two suggestions for alterations in the charter appear frequently and are the two most commonly agreed upon throughout the country.
[23] Biddle to Allen, February 27, 1832, PLB.
[24] Senate Documents, 23rd Congress, 2nd Session, vol. II. But these instructions were not sent until after the Veto.
[25] Knox, p. 355.
[26] House Journal, 22nd Congress, 1st Session, pp. 330, 444, 450, 510.

of both parties, and one of the Jacksonian newspapers in Middlebury was pro-Bank. From Biddle's letter of February 27th we see that Jacksonian friends of the Bank were joining with its enemies in the Jacksonian party, thus giving precedence to Jackson's reelection over agitation of the Bank issue. Complicating the situation a little more is Gammon's report listing Vermont as giving Wirt, the anti-Masonic candidate for president in 1832, the largest popular vote, 13,106 as contrasted with 7,870 for Jackson, and 11,152 for Clay.[27]

We come now to New England's leader, Massachusetts, the spokesman and pacesetter for the Northeast and the alleged heart of pro-Bank sentiment. If Vermont was able to muster 8 state bank memorials from 10 existing state banks, surely Massachusetts with 102 state banks in 1833 [28] might be expected to shower Congress with similar documents. Likewise this state, advanced in commerce and manufacturing, intellectually sophisticated as to the advantages of a strong national bank, and home of Bank advocates of the stature of Webster and Adams, ought to have produced dozens of citizens' petitions. And remembering how heavily the Massachusetts delegation in Congress voted for the Bank, we should not be surprised to discover that the state legislature had forwarded instructions to Washington to vote in support of the Bank. Let us see:

January 16, 1832

Thos. H. Perkins, Esq.[29]
Boston

The Bank having after great consideration presented a memorial to Congress for a renewal of its charter, the Citizens of Philadelphia are sending petitions to that body recommending the measure and a similar memorial will be transmitted by the State Banks. It is so desirable that Congress should be fully informed on the subject that we much wish for the same expression of sentiments among your mer-

---

[27] Gammon, p. 170.   [28] Knox, p. 369.
[29] A director of the Bank in Philadelphia, and the wealthiest resident of Boston.

chants and bankers. . . . Will you do me the favor to talk to our friends, and try to put it in motion? [30]

Biddle sent a letter just like this to B. D. Crowninshield [31] of Salem, Massachusetts.[32] Still another letter reads as follows:

Philadelphia,
January 16, 1832

Gardiner Greene, Esq.[33]
(Private)

My Dear Sir:
The Bank having after great consideration presented a memorial for the renewal of the charter, the citizens of Philadelphia are forwarding petitions on the subject of a similar measure [which] will be transmitted by the State Banks. It would be greatly desirable to have the same thing done elsewhere. I have written today to our friend Col. Perkins and I wish you and our other friends would endeavour to have a strong and general expression of the sense of your community so that Congress may be apprized of the real sentiments of the country.[34]
And finally:

Philadelpha,
January 16, 1832

(Private)
John Parker, Esq.
Boston, Massachusetts

My Dear Sir:
I have written a line to Col. Perkins and another to our friend Mr. Greene on the subject of an expression of opinion from your community and especially from your Banks. . . .[35]

On the 23rd of January Samuel Frothingham, cashier of the

[30] Biddle to Perkins, January 16, 1832, PLB.
[31] A wealthy merchant and on the Board at Philadelphia.
[32] Biddle to Crowninshield, January 16, 1832, PLB.
[33] President of the Boston branch of the Bank. According to McGrane, p. 170, alleged to be the wealthiest citizen of Boston as quoting Justin Winsor (ed.), *Memorial Hist. of Boston*, vol. IV, pp. 29, 30.
[34] Biddle to Greene, January 16, 1832, PLB.
[35] Biddle to Parker, January 16, 1832, PLB.

Boston branch, sent to McIlvaine, the cashier of the Bank at Philadelphia, a copy of a memorial from the friends of the Bank. He says that the opposition has gotten up a memorial requesting a new national bank, at the demise of the Second United States Bank, to be located in Boston with a capital of $50,000,000. They are willing to pay the General Government one per cent on the capital and a tax to the State wherever a branch is located which will be equal to the tax which the banks of the State may pay.[36]

Perkins answered Biddle the same day: ". . . it is doubtful whether the Directors of the Banks, *as such*, would give their signatures. It has been thought better to receive the names of Directors of the local banks in their individual capacity, rather than to apply to their boards. The papers will be sent to Salem . . . and forwarded to Webster." [37]

From P. P. Degrand, a close friend of Biddle's in Boston, came a letter written on January 30th. He tells of the request for a new Bank being circulated and says that it has the most respectable signatures on it. There are two lists of names—one headed by Josiah Thorndike, who had had a difficulty with Biddle, and the other headed by David Henshaw,[38] a true-blue Jackson leader who also had had some contention with the United States Bank Board there in Boston. The list of names will be as surprising to Biddle as it is to Degrand.

The petition in favor of the Bank does not seem to be producing similar enthusiasm. Could not Webster, Silsbee, Edward Everett, and Dearborn [39] write from Washington to Perkins, A. H. Everett,[40] Gideon Barstow, Sprague,[41] and others to say

[36] Frothingham to McIlvaine, January 23, 1832, NBP.
[37] Perkins to Biddle, January 23, 1832, NBP.
[38] The David Henshaw petition was reported as presented to the Senate by William Marcy of New York in Niles' *Register*, January 26, 1832.
[39] Congressmen from Massachusetts.
[40] Editor of the *National Quarterly Review* and brother of Edward Everett in Congress.
[41] State of Massachusetts legislators.

how important it is from every point of view that *"Massachusetts move in a solid Phalanx for the Bank?"*

The memorial in favor of renewing the Bank's charter is felt by Degrand to be a *feeble* production, using none of the strong arguments and simply saying that the Bank is well conducted and useful. It does not even mention that a *new* United States Bank *will not* be, at first, equally useful—nor does it give the view of distress that will occur from non-renewal.

Degrand adds a postscript saying that since the legislature of Massachusetts is in session, and if the advice of their friends in Washington can be made to produce in favor of the Bank, there might be a vote of either the legislature or a legislative caucus of the members of the National Republican Party—this might give a tone and direction to persons who headlessly sign and may sign for a new national bank. Degrand urges that Webster and Silsbee see Pearse and Burgess of Rhode Island and ask them to write home. Let Dearborn write Jarvis of Vermont and Bishop of New Haven, Connecticut.[42]

What do the Congressional records show as the end product of this lengthy correspondence and subsequent effort? Of about 102 state banks only 4—the Bank of Grafton, in Haverhill, the Bank of Bunker's Hill, the Bank of Concord, and the Bank of Lowell [43] sent memorials. There was one citizens' memorial in favor of the Bank and this came from Boston.[44] Three memorials were presented to Congress: one from Lynn, another from William Bartlet and the citizens of Newburyport, and one from Boston, all asking that at the extinction of the Bank they might have a new national bank located in that area.[45] No instructions were received from the state legislature.

What can we conclude about Massachusetts? It did give the Bank support in the most final sense, i.e., its legislators in Wash-

[42] Degrand to Biddle, January 30, 1832, NBP.
[43] *House Journal*, 22nd Congress, 1st Session, pp. 436, 899.
[44] *House Journal*, 22nd Congress, 1st Session, p. 286.
[45] House Journal, 22nd Congress, 1st Session, pp. 331, 385.

ington all voted in favor of the recharter.[46] Biddle's letters sound as though he had little question or hesitancy about requesting their support. Yet apparently Massachusetts did not feel sufficiently pro-Bank to respond in the sense that many states in the South and West did, or as forcefully as Vermont.

There is a letter in the manuscripts which suggests an explanation for this attitude in Massachusetts. On June 7, 1831, Biddle wrote to Thomas Perkins at the Boston office recommending that since business has fallen off so badly there the discount rate should be dropped to 5 per cent. But he cautions Perkins to do it quietly.[47]

It will be recalled that the memorial from the Bank of Amherst [48] referred to a recent oversupply of capital in Boston which had forced the interest rate down to 4½ per cent. This, together with Biddle's letter, raises the question of just how important *was* the Bank to Massachusetts. Looking at the circulation in Massachusetts of state bank notes in 1833, we find they amounted to $7,889,110.[49] On April 4, 1832, the amount of United States Bank notes in circulation there was only $264,720,[50] or about 3 per cent of the circulation of the state banks. This ratio of United States notes to state bank notes was the lowest to be found in any of the states. This was not a new situation; and it had obtained there for many years. In 1823 the note circulation of the state banks amounted to $3,128,986,[51] and the United States Bank note circulation only $172,595,[52] or about 5½ per cent. Clearly, Massachusetts did not depend on the United States Bank notes for its principal medium of exchange as did many of the southwestern and western states. Massachusetts did not need the Bank for the disciplinary benefits of its capacity to keep the note issues of the state banks of Massachusetts or of

[46] See Map 1, p. 8.   [47] Biddle to Perkins, June 7, 1831, PLB.
[48] See Bank of Amherst memorial, p. 69.   [49] Knox, p. 369.
[50] *Senate Documents*, 23rd Congress, 2nd Session vol. II, doc. 17.
[51] Knox, p. 369.
[52] *Senate Documents*, 23rd Congress, 2nd Session, vol. II, doc. 17.

New England within bounds. It had a very efficient system of its own to perform this function, the Suffolk Banking System.[53] Maine, New Hampshire, and Connecticut operated under this system, and Vermont in 1831 adopted the New York Safety Fund system. The Bank as a source of loans and discounts (we know from Biddle's letter to Perkins) was not important to Massachusetts. And from the memorial of the Bank of Amherst it appears that there was a surplus of capital in Boston.

All in all, then, the economic gains which the Bank was able to provide for other sections of the country were not needed by Massachusetts. Apparently, the motivation to provide enthusiastic appeals in support of the Bank was lacking in the absence of any anticipated immediate and painful economic loss to be suffered should the Bank not be rechartered. Just how crucial this negative behavior on the part of Massachusetts was to the history of the Bank will become clearer later on. For the moment it is sufficient to recognize that the state commonly thought of as the heart of pro-Bank sentiment was unable to rally any strength to the support of the Bank.[54]

As for Rhode Island, we have little information. Neither is there correspondence between Biddle and the branch in Providence at this time, nor do congressional records show any memorials received from state banks, citizens' groups, or the state legislature.[55] In Degrand's letter [56] it was anticipated that if this

[53] The Suffolk Bank of Boston agreed to redeem free of interest the notes of any country bank which would make with it a permanent deposit of at least $2,000, the size of the deposit depending upon the capital and business of the country bank. In addition, the country banks were required to keep an amount above the permanent deposit sufficient to cover the bills which came into the possession of the Suffolk Bank. Should the amount redeemed exceed the deposit above and beyond the permanent deposit, the Suffolk Bank charged interest. Should the amount redeemed exceed the permanent deposit, the Suffolk Bank reserved the right of sending home the bills for specie redemption.

[54] Except, of course, from the state's delegation in Congress.

[55] Records of Rhode Island's state legislature cannot be used since they are available only from the year 1905 on. See Grace E. MacDonald, *Check-list of Legislative Journals of the States of the United States of America* (Providence: Oxford press, 1938).

[56] See above, p. 75.

state were spurred on by its Representatives in the House in Washington, it would produce evidence of Bank support. Whether or not Pearse and Burgess took action is not known. At any rate, we may conclude that there was no spontaneous outburst of effort in Rhode Island on behalf of the Bank.

Connecticut, in contrast, provides a great deal of information by which to understand its attitude toward the Bank.

Enoch Parsons, president of the Bank's branch in Hartford, was a man with whom Biddle frequently corresponded and whom he apparently trusted. For example, in February of 1831, when the New York legislature was threatening to pass a resolution against the Bank, Biddle was very anxious to prevent this and Parsons was the man who acted as his agent. From Biddle's experience as a member of the Pennsylvania state legislature at the time the First United States Bank petitioned for renewal of its charter, he believed many members might vote against the Bank from just sheer ignorance of banking. To counteract such a possibility in New York, he asked Parsons to go to Albany and try to instruct those members of the legislature who were uninformed about the functions of the Bank.[57]

Parsons ought to have been one of the first men to whom Biddle would write at the time he began soliciting memorials in support of the Bank. We have seen that the bulk of these letters were written on January 16, 1832. But Biddle waited until January 28th to write Parsons; by which time answers had already been received by him from other parts of the country in response to his requests of the 16th. Also curious is the fact that Biddle limited his request in this case to state banks and simply asked whether they would send memorials, making no mention of either citizens' or state legislature memorials.[58]

Two earlier letters written by Parsons in February of 1831

[57] Biddle to Parsons, February 7, 1831, PLB. This was the February preceding the New York State April 6th and April 9th votes recorded on Maps 3 and 4.
[58] Biddle to Parsons, January 28, 1832, PLB.

give some insight into the situation. On February 25, 1831, Enoch Parsons wrote that the Connecticut people are heavily engaged in manufacturing, and hence derive great benefits from the Bank which the state banks cannot give.[59] A few weeks later he again wrote to inform Biddle that both political parties in Connecticut are confident of success. If the administration party wins, there will be a motion against the renewal of the Bank's charter. But Parsons feels that the administration party will probably fail in Connecticut.[60]

Remembering that the Connecticut delegates voted 100 per cent in favor of the Bank, it may be that Biddle felt relatively certain of both the legislature and the people who had elected them. But when it came to the state banks, he was hesitant. Biddle's request of the 28th and a letter from Parsons to Biddle must have crossed, for Parsons' is also dated the 28th. In it he reports a rumor to Biddle that as a result of instructions from Washington, some large stockholders in the local banks have held a secret meeting to get up a resolution for Congress against the Bank. He admits that he does not know whether this is true, but he will nevertheless get up a countermovement.[61]

Here we have the first instance of a memorial against the Bank initiated independently of action started by the Bank's supporters. This letter also indicates, as has been pointed out, that the Bank's opponents in Washington were making an effort to secure anti-Bank memorials.

By February 4th Parsons had confirmed the rumors about the anti-Bank meeting. He wrote Biddle that sundry resolutions have been passed,[62] but of the 150 men attending the meeting, only twenty or thirty voted. A memorial has been sent by them to Congress. It is Parsons' opinion that the state banks will not

[59] Parsons to Biddle, February 25, 1831, NBP. See p. 82 for explanation of why manufacturing benefited more from the Bank than from state banks.
[60] Parsons to Biddle, March 11, 1831, NBP.
[61] Parsons to Biddle, January 28, 1832, NBP.
[62] Parsons to Biddle, February 4, 1832, NBP.

give memorials, but he promises to try in other towns. He goes on to say that the anti-Bank meeting has been generally frowned upon and that a favorable memorial is presently being signed by gentlemen of *"first standing"* in addition to mercantilists and businessmen. Parsons thinks the insurance offices will cooperate and are *with* the Bank. Those attending the anti-Bank meeting were:

÷	Ward Woodbridge	Director of the Phenix Bank, Hartford
×	Albert Day	Director of the Phenix Bank, Hartford
÷	Samuel Tudor	Director of the Phenix Bank, Hartford
÷	George Beach	Cashier of the Phenix Bank, Hartford
×	Eliph. Averill	Director of the Connecticut River Bank
×	H. Alden	Cashier of the Connecticut River Bank
	H. E. Perkins	Cashier of the Hartford Bank
×	J. M. Niles	Postmaster and editor of the *Times*
×	J. Perkins	
×	H. L. Ellsworth	
×	Rupell	Printer of the *Times*

÷ Clay men.   × Jackson men.

We know from other evidence that the men who actually signed the memorial were Tudor, Averill, Alden, Perkins, and Ellsworth, four of five being connected with state banks and four of five being Jacksonians.[63]

On February 8th Parsons sent Biddle a memorial of the Fire Insurance Company of Hartford which was pro-Bank. Also enclosed was a memorial signed by 400 to 500 of the principal inhabitants. Next week he plans to send another. Parsons goes on to say that the state banks do not want the Bank, but they believe they will have one. If so, they want some changes in the charter "for the protection of local banks." [64]

Here, finally, is definite evidence that some state banks were against the Bank together with a positive act taken principally by state bank officers.

[63] *Executive Documents*, 22nd Congress, 1st Session, vol. IV, doc. 107.
[64] Parsons to Biddle, February 8, 1832, NBP.

Actually presented to Congress was this memorial, three pro-Bank memorials from the Bank of Windham in Windsor, the Thames Bank, and the Bank of Norwich, both in Norwich; a favorable memorial from the Fire Insurance Company of Hartford, another from Merchants and Others of Hartford, and one from the citizens of Stonington.[65]

Two puzzling questions present themselves immediately. What did Parsons mean in his letter of February 25, 1831, when he said that the Bank gave the manufacturing interests in Connecticut something the state banks could not give? Second, why should insurance companies support the Bank?

For the answer to the first question we must refer to the memorial of the citizens of Boston previously mentioned but not discussed.[66] The memorial is conventional and dull except for the section which says that the mercantile, manufacturing, and other classes in the community derive benefits from the Bank not afforded by state banks; i.e., the Bank transfers from place to place throughout the country funds necessary for the purchase of the great staples of the South and West. Internal commerce flows easily as a result.

The memorial of the Fire Insurance Company of Hartford states that since its business extends over many states of the Union, it needs the facilities of the Bank. The branches of the Bank make possible the speedy transfer of payments to those suffering losses.[67] The memorial from the "Merchants and Others" of Hartford also refers to the help afforded them in their business transactions at distant points.[68]

It was the convenience, then, offered by the location and system of branches of the Bank which was appreciated by these groups of merchants, manufacturers, and insurance compan-

[65] *House Journal*, 22nd Congress, 1st Session, pp. 331, 474, 534. *Senate Documents*, 22nd Congress, 1st Session, vol. II, doc. 86. *Executive Documents*, 22nd Congress, 1st Session, vol. IV, doc. 108, 112.
[66] See Boston memorial, p. 75.
[67] *Executive Documents*, 22nd Congress, 1st Session, vol. IV, doc. 112.
[68] *Executive Documents*, 22nd Congress, 1st Session, vol. IV, doc. 108.

ies—anyone whose business was not confined simply to one lo-
cality and who had to pay out money at distant points.

There were in Connecticut in 1834 about twenty-eight state
banks.[69] Hence, three pro-Bank memorials was a very poor
showing of support. This fact, together with Enoch Parsons' letters and the memorial signed by state bank officers, seems to indicate that most of the state banks of Connecticut were hostile
to the Bank. But what can be said of the area as a whole? The
delegates in Congress gave unanimous support, as shown by
their votes, although there is no record of the state legislature instructing them to do so. We know from Parsons that the Bank
question had, as early as the end of February 1831, become a political issue, the administration party being opposed to the Bank.
But to what extent?

Of those attending the anti-Bank meeting we know three
were Clay men and seven Jackson men, so that although the issue was not completely a party one it was rather heavily so. In
1832 Connecticut gave Clay 17,519 votes, Jackson 11,041, and
Wirt 3,335.[70] Does this give us the right to conclude that the
people were pro-Bank? Strictly speaking, no. But we are not
told explicitly, as was the case in Maine and New Hampshire,
that the enemies of the Bank were sufficiently strong to prohibit
action on the part of its supporters. Also, in general the anti-
Bank meeting lacked popular support; in fact was "frowned
on," and only twenty or thirty of 150 attending voted. If we
consider further that Connecticut was heavily engaged in manufacturing, and that this group along with other businessmen tes-
tified to the benefits of the Bank, it would be fair to guess that
the support of Connecticut's citizens fell somewhat to the side of
the Bank.

Nothing has been said so far about requests for branches in
New England. Of a total of sixty-six requests for branches
which were refused, only seven came from New England—one

[69] Knox, p. 387.   [70] Gammon, p. 170.

from Bangor in Maine, one from Concord in New Hampshire, two from Vermont; Middlebury and Brandon (both on the trade route to Canada), one from Bristol, Rhode Island, one from New Bedford in Massachusetts, and one from New Haven in Connecticut. These few requests present a striking contrast to the forty-four petitioned for in the South and West, and again suggests about New England as a whole what was earlier concluded about Massachusetts: that this part of the country did not need the Bank in any of the basic senses that the South and West did.

Making the same comparison for the other New England states as was made for Massachusetts, we find that the ratio of United States Bank notes in circulation to the state bank notes was only one to ten in Maine, New Hampshire, Rhode Island, and Connecticut. Unfortunately the Bank note circulation for Burlington, Vermont, on April 4, 1832, is not given in the Senate Documents of the 23rd Congress, 2nd Session. But the five states for which we do have figures show a sharp contrast to the South and West where, except for two or three states, the ratio ran upwards of one to two.

To sum up the situation in the Northeast: Maine must be counted against the Bank. Its state and national legislators were anti-Bank; the state legislature went so far as to instruct the delegation in Congress to vote against renewal, and a majority of the congressmen followed instructions. Among Maine's citizens there was more sentiment against the Bank than for it, otherwise demonstrations in support of the Bank could not have been silenced.

New Hampshire must also be considered against the Bank, but strangely enough, this does not hold true for the state banks. As to the citizens, we are explicitly told by Jeremiah Mason that those supporting the Bank were superior in wealth, character, and respectability, but fewer in numbers.[71]

Massachusetts presents an unexpected picture—the congres-

[71] See Mason's letter, p. 67.

sional representatives supporting the Bank but a pitiful showing of memorials from both state banks and citizens. The three hostile petitions requesting that the Boston area be made the location of a new national bank suggest that "Wall Street's jealousy of Chestnut Street" should read "Boston's jealousy of Philadelphia."

As for Rhode Island, there were no memorials either requesting renewal or opposing it.

Connecticut shows a mixed picture, the state banks being hostile, the national legislators favorable, and the citizens probably more favorable than hostile.

Lastly, Vermont must be counted pro-Bank on all sides, state legislature and national representatives, the citizens, the state banks.

When just the question of the state banks is considered, the only positive evidence of hostility is in Connecticut. On the other hand, the state banks of both New Hampshire and Vermont gave strong support to the Bank.

As to areas of strong support—only Vermont can be claimed.

Comparing the South and West with the Northeast, we find that the two areas seem to have exchanged their conventional roles. The numerous citizens' memorials, the high percentage of state banks that petitioned for renewal, the many requests for new branches, and the superior quality of the contents of the memorials from the South, Southwest, and West are all representative of the strength of support associated with our ideas of New England. Similarly, the limited support, the apathy, and the open hostility exhibited by New England are reminiscent of our traditional ideas of the South, Southwest, and the West. It must be admitted, however, that the exchange of roles makes better economic sense. Where the Bank was desperately needed, for a variety of reasons, it was wanted with enthusiasm. But where its function was limited mainly to the smooth transfer of funds, it was at best just tolerated.

7

The Middle States

WITH THE EXCEPTION of New York, the last group of states we will consider, the Middle states, may be quickly disposed of. Two of them, Delaware and New Jersey, had no branches of the Second United States Bank and consequently little correspondence exists about them.

In fact, there is no correspondence at all about Delaware. All we know is that the state legislature requested Congress to vote in favor of renewal.[1] This Delaware's legislators in both the United States Senate and House of Representatives did unanimously.[2] We also know that there was a request to locate a branch in Wilmington.[3] Two state bank memorials in favor of the Bank were sent by the Bank of Delaware [4] and the Bank of Smyrna.[5] Knox spoke of only one state bank [6] prior to 1832, The Farmer's Bank, and listed but three banks in existence as of 1836.[7]

From this evidence we would have to consider Delaware's state banks friendly. There is also no reason to suppose the state as a whole to have been otherwise.

As to New Jersey—one of Biddle's most trusted advisers on both political and financial matters, Roswell L. Colt, wrote from Paterson on November 10, 1832, that he expects an expression of the state legislature in favor of a branch,[8] a prediction cor-

---

[1] *House Journal*, 22nd Congress, 1st Session, p. 286.   [2] See Map 1 on p. 8.
[3] *Senate Documents*, 23rd Congress, 2nd Session, vol. II, doc. 17.
[4] *Senate Journal*, 22nd Congress, 1st Session, p. 70.
[5] *Senate Journal*, 22nd Congress, 1st Session, p. 154.
[6] John J. Knox, *A History of Banking in the United States* (New York: B. Rhodes and Company, 1900), pp. 467–68.
[7] Knox, p. 468.   [8] Colt to Biddle, November 10, 1832, NBP.

roborated by P. Dickerson.[9] There was in fact a resolution before the New Jersey General Assembly to request the establishment of a branch of the Bank in New Jersey.[10] John Potter
communicated with Colt and lets him know that New Jersey's
senators and representatives will support renewal of the Bank's
charter.[11] As we know, he was correct, for New Jersey voted
unanimously for the Bank in June, 1832.[12] A note in Colt's
handwriting announces: "We have got our country banks at
work and these will throw into Congress memorial after memorial." [13]

Three state bank memorials are recorded as having been presented to Congress: the Bank of Camden, the Trenton Banking
Company, and the Cumberland Bank in Bridgeton.[14] What
happened to Colt's "country banks" is undetermined. However, Niles' *Register* of January 27th reported that Mr. Freling-
huysen, senator from New Jersey, presented to the Senate resolutions from the Bank of New Jersey recommending the renewal of the charter of the Bank. Two requests were made for
branches, one from Paterson and the other from Newark.[15]

We may conclude, as in the case of Delaware, that New Jersey offers no evidence of state bank hostility nor unfriendliness
on the part of its citizens.

Since there was a branch of the Bank in Baltimore, more is
known about Maryland than about the preceding two states.
John Leeds Kerr, a representative from Easton, Maryland,
wrote Biddle on December 27, 1831, from Washington declar-
ing that Maryland's sentiments are so pro-Bank, that no mem-

---

[9] The brother of Mahlon Dickerson, senator from New Jersey, previously
mentioned as pro-Bank but who voted against the Bank.
[10] New Jersey Journal of the General Assembly [Votes and Proceedings] 1st
Sitting of the 56th General Assembly, p. 108.
[11] Potter to Colt, February 8, 1832, NBP.   [12] See Map 1, p. 8.
[13] Colt to Biddle, about March 1, 1832, NBP.
[14] *House Journal*, 22nd Congress, 1st Session. Also see the *New York American Advocate*, January 20, 1832, p. 1.
[15] *Senate Documents*, 23rd Congress, 2nd Session, vol. II, doc. 17.

ber of Congress will vote against it,[16] and the following day Thomas Cadwalader wrote to much the same effect.[17]

Two days after sending the Bank's petition for renewal to Congress, Nicholas Biddle informs Josiah Bayly, Cambridge, Maryland, what he has done. He has done it even while aware that the friends of Jackson do not want the issue raised now because of its possible effect on the election. Biddle declares that he cannot yield to this argument, for it will break the Bank's position of political neutrality.[18] Then on the 16th Biddle asks William Patterson, president of the branch in Baltimore, Robert Oliver, another very close adviser, and George Hoffman, a director of the Baltimore and Ohio Railroad, for both citizens' memorials and state bank memorials.[19]

John McKim wrote on the 17th (their letters must have crossed) to let Biddle know that the Maryland legislature will pass a memorial to Congress by a large majority. He adds that the state banks will be delighted to do the same.[20] He was correct on both counts; Congress received a memorial from the legislature [21] and memorials from five state banks in Baltimore.[22] Altogether only twelve banks are mentioned as existing in the whole state of Maryland in 1830, and in 1834 only eight are listed; [23] so the state banks made a very good showing.[24]

Maryland's demand for capital was somewhere between New

[16] Kerr to Biddle, December 27, 1831, NBP.

[17] Cadwalader to Biddle, January 28, 1831, NBP.

[18] Biddle to Bayly, January 9, 1832, PLB.

[19] Biddle to Patterson, Biddle to Oliver, Biddle to Hoffman, January 16, 1832, PLB.

[20] McKim to Biddle, January 17, 1832, NBP.

[21] *House Journal*, 22nd Congress, 1st Session, p. 258. Also see the *New York American Advocate*, January 20, 1832, reporting the passage of a resolution by the state Senate in favor of renewal of the Bank's charter.

[22] *House Journal*, 22nd Congress, 1st Session, pp. 385, 413, 444, 510. *Senate Documents*, 22nd Congress, 1st Session, vol. I, doc. 48. These were the Marine Bank, Mechanics Bank, Bank of Baltimore, the Commercial and Farmers' Bank, and the Franklin Bank.

[23] Knox, pp. 467, 497, 518.

[24] In Stuart Bruchey's edition of Taney's manuscript on the Baltimore pet banks in the *Maryland Historical Magazine*, 1958, p. 136, it is said that all banks, except two, were in the hands of people friendly to the Bank.

England's and that of the Southwest and West; Maryland had some of her own but not enough. According to Knox:

The whole state was dependent for bank accommodations upon twelve banks of which eight were in Baltimore. The total capital for the state was $5,455,000, exclusive of the $1,500,000 to $2,000,000 employed by the branch of the United States Bank. The counties needed the introduction of facilities at the more advanced points, and the city needed an increased banking capital.[25]

A memorial to this effect from Charles Carroll of Carrollton and 2,200 signers—merchants and other citizens of Baltimore, was presented to Congress.[26]

Maryland's attitude, state banks, citizens, and legislature, is appropriately summed up by Robert Oliver in a letter to Biddle dated February 11, 1832: "Nearly the whole of our people have been warm friends of your bank." [27]

As might have been anticipated, Pennsylvania, the home of the Bank, offers almost no evidence of opposition.

Biddle once again is warned, however, on November 3, 1831, by Silas Burroughs [28] in New York. He writes that the Pennsylvania delegation is presently in the City, and that one of its members, Judge William Wilkins,[29] thinks the question of recharter should not be raised this session. The people of Pennsylvania feel this will interfere with the President's election.[30] Nonetheless, on January 16th Biddle wrote the Pittsburgh branch of the Bank a letter very like his letter to Jeremiah Mason [31] of Portsmouth, stating the action that the state banks of Pennsylvania are taking [32] for the purpose of depriving the Bank's enemies of their most efficient weapon.[33]

[25] Knox, p. 497.
[26] *Senate Documents*, 22nd Congress, 1st Session, vol. I, doc. 47.
[27] Oliver to Biddle, February 11, 1832, NBP.
[28] A well-known New Yorker who had offered to do anything for the Bank that he could.
[29] A member of the United States House of Representatives.
[30] Burroughs to Biddle, November 3, 1831, NBP.
[31] See Mason's letter, p. 67.
[32] I.e., forwarding pro-Bank memorials to Congress.
[33] Biddle to Conery, January 16, 1832, PLB.

The interesting insight to be had from the Pennsylvania correspondence is a recognition of the weight and importance attached to their instructions to Congress by the state legislatures of both Pennsylvania and New York. There are several letters centering on this point but one from Charles Jared Ingersoll captures the essence of the matter. To offset the New York resolution against the Bank, he writes, Pennsylvania must produce a heavy majority on the opposite resolution.[34]

J. B. Wallace, a member of the Pennsylvania state legislature, wrote Biddle that the Bank resolution was introduced into both branches of the legislature on February 3rd, passing the House 77-7 and the Senate unanimously.[35] This was considered a great triumph for the Bank and for Biddle, as is evident from the many letters he wrote informing people of this overwhelming pro-Bank majority, using it to help persuade others to follow suit. To understand the full significance of the resolution it must be remembered that Pennsylvania at this period was a Jacksonian state, the Democrats representing a heavy majority in both the Pennsylvania delegation to Congress and in the state legislature. Biddle himself had voted for Jackson in 1828 and would not allow himself to be classed as a National Republican.[36] It is striking, then, that pro-Bank instructions to Congress should have been voted for almost unanimously in so powerful a Democratic state as Pennsylvania.

The Pennsylvania banks rallied to the support of the Bank, record having been kept of fifteen memorials from them.[37] Knox listed forty-one banks in existence in 1834 [38] though it

[34] Ingersoll to Biddle, January 31, 1832, NBP.
[35] Wallace to Biddle, February 3, 1832, NBP.
[36] Edward Everett, a National-Republican representative from Massachusetts, wrote Biddle on April 25, 1831, to introduce to him Dr. S. G. Howe of Boston. He says that Howe is a Clay man and adds that even though Biddle will not permit Everett to class him as a "Clay man," they will enjoy meeting each other. Everett to Biddle, April 25, 1831, NBP.
[37] *House Journal*, 22nd Congress, 1st Session, pp. 186, 225, 258, 286, 330, 385, 412, 413.
[38] Knox, p. 462.

should be kept in mind that expansion of state banks was enormous between 1832 and 1834, after Jackson had vetoed the bill to recharter the Bank.

Citizens' memorials were sent from Philadelphia, Delaware County, and from the "manufacturers, mechanics and merchants in Pittsburgh and adjacent parts." [39] Dallas presented four memorials from the "traders to the West and others." [40]

Curiously enough, there was one anti-Bank memorial sent from the citizens of Pittsburgh urging that the charter not be renewed because of the Bank's being a monopoly and unconstitutional. It continues in its rather stereotyped way to say that too many foreigners are involved in the ownership of the stock of the Bank.[41] Incidentally, Thomas Benton of Missouri, leader of the anti-Bank fight in the Senate, presented this memorial in that chamber whereas two favorable memorials from Albany, New York, were presented by George McDuffie of South Carolina, leader of the pro-Bank sentiment in the House. Earlier [42] attention was called to the fact that William Marcy presented David Henshaw's memorial. Ordinarily it was the custom for congressmen from the states issuing the memorials to present them. But in the case of the four documents mentioned above—two anti-Bank memorials from the foremost pro-Bank states, Pennsylvania and Massachusetts, and two pro-Bank memorials from an area believed to be the seat of opposition—special care was taken in their presentation to make the most of each.

Two very interesting letters throw still further light on state bank attitudes. Robinson of Virginia wrote Biddle on July 16, 1831, that he has seen a letter from Mr. Girard [43] of Philadelphia to a friend in New York saying what a misfortune it will be

[39] *House Journal,* 22nd Congress, 1st Session, pp. 450, 534. *Senate Documents,* 22d Congress, 1st Session, vol. II, doc. 171.

[40] *Senate Journal,* 22nd Congress, 1st Session, pp. 78, 81, 91, 94.

[41] *Senate Journal,* 22nd Congress, 1st Session, p. 257.

[42] See Henshaw's memorial, p. 75, footnote 38.

[43] The famous merchant and banker, Stephen Girard.

if the charter of the Bank is not renewed. The state banks will in a very short time be forced to suspend specie. Girard adds that as a *banker* he will be better off if the United States Bank is not rechartered, but as a merchant he will not. Robinson adds that unfortunately Girard's opinion will influence the state banks.[44]

Here, possibly, is a piece of evidence for believing state banks hostile to the Bank. However, it is doubtful that either Girard's statements came to be known to other state banks as widely as Robinson believed they would be, or true that his position was typical. Girard had very good reason to have maintained a friendly relation with the Bank, and at the same time to have felt the threat of the Bank most acutely, if we may judge from a letter written by Biddle to Cadwalader at the time of Girard's death. Biddle wrote that when Girard died his bank's books showed the following disgraceful situation:

Discounts	$3,300,000
Circulation	200,000
Debt to B.U.S.	140,000
Specie	16,000

Biddle does not know the amount of deposits, but thinks they must have been at least some hundreds of thousands, yet the specie in the bank's vault was only $16,000. Everyone thought Girard kept $300,000 to $500,000 on hand.[45]

At the time of Stephen Girard's death his bank had applied to the United States Bank for a loan of $100,000, which Biddle instantly granted, and this was not the first time Biddle had come to Girard's aid for a similar amount. Hence, although the ridiculously low quantity of specie put Girard in extreme peril of suspension, Biddle apparently never pressed him. On the contrary, he generously accommodated Girard. Under these circumstances it is doubtful Girard would have broadcast the statement that as a banker he was better off, if the Bank's charter

[44] Robinson to Biddle, July 16, 1831, NBP.
[45] Biddle to Cadwalader, December 29, 1831, NBP.

were not renewed. As was previously stated, his position was not typical of most eastern big city bankers. They did not usually operate with so little specie in relation to their circulation and hence would not have felt the influence of the Bank to the extent that Girard must have felt it.[46]

NEW YORK STATE

As was indicated in the first chapter, the situation in New York State with respect to the Bank was of such a nature that little insight is to be gained by treating the state as a whole as has been done with the other states. To say that only one state bank of the forty-one [47] in existence in 1831 sent a favorable memorial, but that about forty memorials from citizens poured in [48] is to present a striking contrast about which more needs to be known.

We have already seen that New York State as a whole voted against the Bank.[49] Though this told us something, not until the votes were analyzed did a pattern develop. Clearly defined areas emerged which were strongly pro-Bank, namely western New York State and New York City. That pattern will be investigated further in the present chapter.

The problem has three principal aspects: far western New York State, Albany, and New York City. However, it is neither possible to separate the correspondence into three geographical areas and take up each area in turn (the same event often had different repercussions in each area), nor does the correspondence lend itself to separating the state bank problem from the

[46] The state banks taken as a whole had a circulation of $68,000,000, and $10,000,000 or $11,000,000 in specie in 1833 according to Catterall, p. 432.

[47] Forty-one is the figure mentioned by Albert Gallatin. Gallatin to Biddle, February 17, 1831, NBP.

[48] *House Journal*, 22nd Congress, 1st Session, pp. 286, 330, 412, 444, 450, 510, 534.

[49] In addition to the resolutions of 1831, on January 24, 1832, the state Senate voted again against renewal of the charter. See *New York American Advocate*, January 28, 1832.

larger problem of a single geographic area so as to first permit an analysis of the state banks. The three areas must be taken together, using the Biddle Manuscripts and the President's Letter Book arranged chronologically.

In a letter to John Watmough,[50] Biddle defends the Bank against the criticism made in the House of Representatives that the branches had multiplied too rapidly. These branches were established in response to requests from the people of the states, or the state legislatures. He then lists several branches and shows the conditions under which they were established. To show how the Bank has resisted opening branches, Biddle enclosed two documents. One was a letter of August 15, 1821, from General Andrew Jackson requesting a branch in Pensacola; and the other, dated July 17, 1826, was a petition for a branch at Albany specially requested by Martin Van Buren, William L. Marcy, Charles E. Dudley, Benjamin Butler, Nathan Sanford, and others of the Regency.[51] James Hamilton also signed. This is rather a surprise, inasmuch as both Jackson and the Albany Regency came to be arch enemies of the Bank. Our concern here is with the petition for a branch at Albany, since this area again requested a branch later on in the period 1831–1832.

The petition states that since the great increase in transportation facilities, Albany has been the entrepôt from West to East and from North to South. Banking capital is so inadequate that people must stand by and watch produce float on past Albany, to New York City. Many merchants would like to be able to buy this produce and reship it. But there is not enough capital, and so it goes to New York City. Albany wants to buy direct, then sell to the home market and ship out whatever the home market cannot absorb. Albany merchants then want to buy a return cargo for interior shipment without the expense of trans-

---

[50] A representative from Pennsylvania.
[51] Biddle to Watmough, May 10, 1832, PLB; see also *Senate Documents*, 23rd Congress, 2nd Session, vol. II, doc. 17.

shipment at New York City and without allowing the profits to go to the importing merchants there.[52]

Apparently the matter was under consideration for some time, but by October of 1826 the request was refused. As later events will show, this may have been one of the most costly decisions Biddle ever made. He wrote of it to Campbell P. White, a Jacksonian Democrat and at the time a director of the New York City branch of the Bank.[53] The tone of the letter suggests that White would be in agreement with the decision. This is surprising since it was the Democrats that requested the branch. White voted against the Bank in 1832, at which time he was a Representative from New York State. The following letter of July 13, 1826, written while he was a director of the Bank in New York City, suggests that his feelings were actually sympathetic to the Bank:

With respect to the combination to which you allude in your last letter: there is no manner of doubt of the existence of such an associaton which has in succession controlled the Franklin Bank, Franklin Fire Insurance Company, the City Bank, the New York Coal Company, The Life and ——[54] Company, the Dutchess County Insurance Company, the Mercantile Insurance Company, the ——[55] Insurance Company, the Fulton Bank, the Morris Canal Bank and lastly the Tradesman's Bank, changing the presidents, cashiers or directors or manipulating them to their *will:* as if by the move of a "magician".[56] Their success which has been remarkable in accomplishing their purposes has at once increased their confidence in their power and their resources for future action, and threatens the peace and harmony of all the respectable institutions. They certainly have acquired an influence to which their wealth, talents or respectability do not entitle them. They now boast their next object is to control the Bank of the United States, stating that on one

---

[52] NBP, about July 17, 1826.   [53] Biddle to White, October, 1826, NBP.
[54] The name is illegible in the manuscript.
[55] The name is illegible in the manuscript.
[56] Whether this is an intentional reference to Van Buren, called the "magician" one cannot be sure.

occasion there were as few as 2,300 votes taken [57] at Philadelphia and that they can, by subdividing their stock in single shares, soon procure such a number of votes as could make any change they might think proper: making the transfers on the *last* day allowed by law to gratify the voter: so as to prevent the possibility of counteracting them. Now, although I view this as an ——[58] thought which they have not the *power* to accomplish, as a warm friend to the present administration of the Bank of the United States and to the safety and well being of the community, I would advise all the means that are within the reach of the Executive of the Institution to be employed to oppose the nefarious plans. I would not permit the Franklin Bank, Fulton Bank, Tradesman's Bank, Morris Canal Bank or the Merchant's Bank to be in debt to the Branch more than 2,000 or 3,000 dollars in the weekly settlement [59] without calling for specie for such balance: *whatever may be the general state of the balances* with the State Banks in this city, and I would not lend or accommodate by discounts on stock or personal security any *person* supposed to belong to their combination. I state for your information what is currently reported, the most monied person in this association is a *late* director of the Bank of the United States with whom you are acquainted, and it is also said that this *person* has obtained large loans from the Bank of the United States at Philadelphia, from the office here and that at Baltimore, which have been employed in this service. This is a mere rumor, but from a newspaper I send you today, you will perceive it is a common opinion.

I have mentioned the Merchants Bank and I should state to you that it is generally believed to bend its will and countenance to the Institutions above named and to the combination by which they are controlled.[60]

Actually the Van Buren petition and White's letter serve mainly as background material for the period under discussion, except for the mention of the City Bank and the Merchants Bank which will appear again.

[57] This refers to votes in proportion to the number of shares of Bank stock owned.

[58] A word is illegible in the manuscript.

[59] This refers to a practice developed by Biddle for settling the balance between the Bank and the state banks with respect to outstanding notes. Biddle wanted this balance kept favorable to the Bank in each of its branches, for this was his principle tool for keeping the state banks' note issues within bounds.

[60] White to Biddle, July 13, 1826, NBP.

Returning to the period in which we are primarily interested: On February 7, 1831, Biddle gathers from the tone of the *Courier and Enquirer* of the previous Saturday that "Washington" has instructed Albany to get the New York State Legislature to prepare a resolution against the Bank. To ward off such action he suggests to the New York City branch that they get a couple of informed Jacksonians to instruct the legislators who are ignorant of the Bank.[61] Here again is an indication that the opposition was campaigning to encourage anti-Bank memorials. Robinson, the cashier of the New York City branch answers that his brother-in-law, John Duer, will do more than anyone in the City to prevent resolutions against the Bank in the state legislature. He is a friend of many leading Jackson men. Mr. Duer has promised to do all he can and will see Livingston and Selden on the subject.[62] Biddle also asks Devereaux, president of the branch in Utica,[63] to go over to Albany and inform the New York State legislature about the Bank, since the Utica people understand its advantages.[64] Finally, he wrote Albert H. Tracy, New York State senator from Erie County, asking whether the New York State legislature will venture to go against the instructions from Washington in regard to the resolution.[65]

We should note that the contemplated legislative action discussed here culminated in the two resolutions voted on in the New York State legislature in April of 1831 and analyzed in Chapter 2. The first resolution referred to indefinite postponement of the Bank question, and when that failed by a vote of 55-55, a few days later a resolution was passed instructing the delegates in Congress to vote against renewal of the Bank's charter.

[61] Biddle to Robinson, February 7, 1831, PLB.

[62] Robinson to Biddle, February 8, 1831 and February 9, 1831, NBP. Livingston and Selden were New York State assemblymen, known to be pro-Bank and Democrats.

[63] The branch of the Bank in Utica had been opened in 1830, the one in Buffalo in 1829.

[64] Biddle to Devereaux, February 7, 1831, PLB. This is the time when he also enlisted the support of Enoch Parsons, referred to earlier, to go over to Albany.

[65] Biddle to Tracy, February 7, 1831, PLB.

Biddle next began to receive reports on the situation in Albany. Silas E. Burrows, who arrived there on or about February 13th, wrote that Mr. Cary, the president of the Genessee Bank and a friend of the Bank of the United States, had told him that he had been asked three times to help in the attack on the Bank.[66] Parsons of Connecticut, however, after talking to many legislators, wrote Biddle that they all favor the Bank and recognize its importance to the State and nation and business community.[67]

Meanwhile, apparently, Biddle had been asked whether the Anti-Masons, the dominant political party of western New York State ought to take a pro-Bank stand at their next convention. Biddle's letter of February 17th to Devereaux, now in Albany, says to let them go ahead and express their opinion. If he interferes and asks them not to, this will be just as much a political act as asking them to speak in the Bank's favor.[68] Biddle also informs Albert Tracy of this and adds that it is acceptable to him because the Anti-Masons are not "political partisans." [69]

Biddle tried all along to keep the Bank from being identified with either political party. He appointed directors from both parties and requested officers of the branches not to engage actively or prominently in political matters. Whenever they did so and he became aware of it, he wrote them, calling attention to the impropriety of their acts. To illustrate: C. C. Cambreleng, a prominent New York State Jacksonian and very much an enemy of the Bank, was a director of the branch in New York City. On May 14, 1829, Biddle found it necessary to write Cambreleng giving him instructions on this very point.[70] This attitude of Biddle's explains, then, his letters to Devereaux and Tracy. It was only because he viewed the Anti-Masonic movement as un-

[66] Burrows to Biddle, February 13, 1831, NBP.
[67] Parsons to Biddle, February 16, 1831, NBP.
[68] Biddle to Devereaux, February 17, 1831, PLB.
[69] Biddle to Tracy, February 17, 1831, PLB.
[70] Biddle to Cambreleng, May 14, 1829, PLB.

political that he permitted the identification of it with the Bank.

By the middle of March Biddle must have felt the need of further reinforcements in Albany, for he wrote Robinson to send Saul Alley, a Jacksonian, up to Albany to enlighten the New York State legislators about the Bank.[71] From Chapter 2 it will be recalled that Assemblyman Morehouse of Otsego County brought up the resolution against the Bank in March of 1831. He must have made a first try on this resolution in early March, for Charles Livingston wrote a letter to Silas Burroughs on March 12th saying that the Morehouse resolution had been brought up without proper party consultation. Some of the members did not want it. If it came up again he, Livingston, would offer additions to it. He warns Burroughs not to be surprised if it passes, or at the way he might vote.[72] A. Bronson, a New York State senator from Oswego County, informs Biddle on March 24th that the resolution has been laid to rest. If it should arise again, it will pass by a "party" vote—only a few men will be willing to disregard party for principle.[73]

It did not take long for the question to be pressed by Morehouse again, and a resolution was brought forward to postpone the question indefinitely. Burrows wrote Biddle of this on April 6th.[74] This motion failed 55-55. Consequently, on April 9th the resolution not to recharter the Bank was voted on and passed by a vote of 73-35. It passed the Senate by a vote of 17-12.

In Chapter 2 we saw that on the first vote New York City gave evidence of very strong pro-Bank feeling by voting for postponement 8-1. It was further pointed out that the New York City vote of 4-3 in favor of the Bank on the second resolution not to recharter the Bank could also be interpreted as indicating strong support, because of a total of eight pro-Bank members who absented themselves rather than change their votes to

[71] Biddle to Robinson, March 18, 1831, NBP.
[72] Livingston to Burroughs, March 12, 1831, NBP.
[73] Bronson to Biddle, March 24, 1831, NBP.
[74] Burroughs to Biddle, April 6, 1831, NBP.

suit the Regency, four of them came from the city. Two letters from Burroughs support both points. After the second vote, he wrote Biddle that great pressure was exerted after the 55-55 vote. The Assembly adjourned even though it had met but one hour before. He points out that the Regency was disappointed over the City, and adds, "most of our members remained true." The following day he wrote again and mentions the Regency's annoyance at the City for holding true to the Bank.[75] By April 12th, the date of his last letter, the Senate had voted and both New York City senators had voted pro-Bank.

At just about this time, April 18th, a very revealing letter was sent to Biddle from S. DeWitt Bloodgood in Albany. Because of its importance, it is quoted almost in full:

The resolution to nullify the United States Bank charter passed our legislature by a slim majority. Even those who made the most violent attacks upon it confessed out of doors that they were compelled to do so by violence of party feeling. I know there are thousands of Jacksonians who supported the present administration out of the purest and most disinterested feelings who cannot and will not barter away the independence of their principles. These men look with horror on the scenes of extortion and unrestrained circulation which an unsettled local currency created, and they resent that such ——[76] views should be entertained of the great questions of political and commercial economy as have been entertained by their own party. The head and fount of the opposition to the United States Bank *here* are to be found in the Cashier of the Mechanics and Farmers' Bank of this City, Mr. Olcott. He is a man decidely unpopular with not a spotless character, if we regard the moral code as a standard of purity. He has, it is thought, extraordinary talents as a financier, and the dividends of the bank which he manages are enormous. A year since, 50 per cent of surplus was declared on the stock of the Company. He manages the business of the bank almost exclusively and by allowing certain persons peculiar advantages in the institution has ——[77] more influence on legislative deliberations than any other person I

---

[75] Burroughs to Biddle, April 11, 1831, and April 12, 1831, NBP.
[76] A word is illegible in the manuscript.   [77] A word is illegible.

know of. Benjamin Knower,[78] formerly Treasurer of the State, a hat-maker and dealer in wool, has acquired a large fortune through the judicious use of the capital of this bank. Mr. Knower and the Bank elevated Mr. Marcy [79] to the adj. Generalship, Comptrollership, then Judgeship of the Supreme Court and now Senatorship, U. S. Senate. Mr. Marcy is an honorable man, but he married at some disparity of years the daughter of Mr. Knower and will be found violently opposed to the United States Bank. Mr. Dudley,[80] my neighbor and friend, whose confidence I think I have is a large stockholder in the Mechanics' and Farmers' Bank. In private life he is the most upright and honorable of men. He is opposed to the Bank.

Mr. Edmonds of the Assembly was a classmate of mine in college and I know him. His circumstances will, I think, together with his connection with Mr. Olcott, decide as to his course and the reasons of his late opposition. This Bank has the control of the Lockport Bank [81] and the Ithaca Bank and by means of one brother, a cashier, controls the Cherry Valley (Bank) and by another, influences the Canal Bank. By a brother-in-law, Mr. North, Mr. Olcott influences the City Bank of New York—by relations at Hudson, he influences the bank there.

A person by the name of Lot Clark, deeply connected with the Lockport Bank and the speculations in surplus water there,[82] has been here all winter bringing the whole force of his clever management to bear upon this question as well as others. This is the influence you must meet in this city if you wish to prevent the legislature of this State being improperly controlled. Your Utica Cashier and your President there, the latter of whom I have known *almost* from the time he ceased to be a fiddler and dancing master, doesn't have any weight with the public and by the extreme strictness with which they transact business, not known at either New York or Buffalo,[83] they disgust many people.

BUT,

I am surprised the United States Bank at New York under these circumstances, continues to keep its account here with the Mechanics' and Farmers' Bank. This Bank is determined if possible to get rid of

---

[78] Member of the Albany Regency.
[79] Later governor of New York.   [80] Another Regency member.
[81] This bank was just a few miles northeast of the branch of the Bank in Buffalo.
[82] Probably a reference to water power.
[83] Refers to the New York City and Buffalo branches of the Bank.

the United States Branches. It has two senators in Congress.[84] Mr. Knower is to go into our State Senate next winter. Alderman Seymour, a complete tool of the Bank, is to go into the assembly. Now the deposits and business of the United States Bank had better be given to its friends rather than to its intolerant enemy. The directors of the State Bank are friendly to the United States Bank. They, though Jacksonians, do not believe in the propriety of mixing up questions of this kind with *political* considerations that have only a real bearing upon individual interests. This bank has the account of the two branches and if no branch of the United States Bank is to be established here (which would be in my opinion a wise policy) then it is important to strengthen your friends and not place your confidence and give your business to an institution hostile in all its feelings and which it is utterly impossible to conciliate.

Desirous that you should be put in possession of facts so important, I trust this communication to your honor and confidence having no other desire than to counteract any schemes discreditable to the country and contrary to the principles of honor and justice. Nor do I seek to draw you into any correspondence further than agreeable to yourself. Where I am known, I trust my character will place me above suspicion.

With respect

Your humble servant

S. DeWitt Bloodgood [85]

Just a few days later he wrote again:

You may have perceived by the sale of the Mechanics and Farmers and the New York State Bank stocks made yesterday that they realized an enormous advance. . . . The attacks constantly made on the United States Bank by the *Argus* [86] would fall at once before an institution established here as once contemplated. A respectable set of Directors and a fair proportion of business men as cashiers would protect it from the increasing attacks of the Mechanics' and Farmers' Bank. This is now a favorable time to establish your Branch and its arrival here would be hailed as a blessing.

To shew the hostility and forwardness of Mr. Olcott, I was just this moment told that he had ordered the Plates for the Bills of the Buffalo Bank at Philadelphia, *although no distribution of stock has*

---

[84] Dudley and Marcy.   [85] Bloodgood to Biddle, April 18, 1831, NBP.
[86] The *Albany Argus,* the Regency newspaper.

taken place. ———[87] went on with joint funds to subscribe the whole capital once and a half times in order to obtain the stock and counteract the plan, we had heard, of making it a branch of the Mechanics' and Farmers' Bank.[88]

Now as interesting and revealing as all this is, it could not be relied on very heavily were its contents not supported elsewhere. Fortunately, they are so substantiated.

In the letter Biddle wrote to the cashier, Robinson, asking that Saul Alley be sent to Albany he says, "A letter received today from Albany says that Mr. Morehouse's motion was suggested or dictated by Mr. Lot Clark." [89]

On April 23rd Robinson wrote that the Farmers' and Mechanics' Bank in Albany has been active in getting Morehouse's resolution through. The New York City branch keeps its entire account with that bank, and a most desirable account it has been, giving the Farmers' and Mechanics' great advantages over the other state banks. If Biddle agrees, he will remove the account to the State Bank. He will await Biddle's reply.[90]

On April 28th Gulian Verplanck, a prominent Democrat from New York City, wrote Biddle that the resolution in Albany was pushed through by party discipline, and it was hard to do.[91]

Burroughs writes again on April 17th to say that Erastus Root, another well-known Democrat, has helped the Bank a great deal in the New York Senate. Root said, " 'it is *not the farmers or mechanics that lobby against the United States Bank but the state bankers.*' " [92] According to Bray Hammond, Root should have known what he was saying. Hammond referred to him as a well informed upstate agrarian who had long observed the relation between the state banks in New York State and the

---

[87] Four words are illegible.   [88] Bloodgood to Biddle, April 21, 1831, NBP.
[89] See Biddle's letter, p. 99.
[90] Robinson to Biddle, April 23, 1831, NBP.
[91] Verplanck to Biddle, April 28, 1831, NBP.
[92] Burroughs to Biddle, April 17, 1831, NBP

Bank, and had been a friend of both the First and Second United States Banks.[93]

As to the wisdom of Bloodgood's suggestion about starting a branch of the Bank: Some months later, on November 30th, James Watson Webb,[94] en route to Washington wrote Biddle that he had wanted to stop and see him about a branch in Albany, but has been prevented by his wife's illness. In any case, he thinks the question should be weighed well by the Bank before the application is rejected. Webb believes it will strengthen the Bank in New York State by setting up a central power having an interest at least separate from, if not hostile to, the Farmers' and Mechanics' Bank. It will enable very many people in Albany, friendly to the Bank, to come out and avow themselves so without fear of the Farmers' and Mechanics' Bank. Furthermore, it will weaken the power of the Farmers' and Mechanics' in the state and strengthen all those who labor to preserve Nicholas Biddle's institution for the benefit of the country. Mr. Noah [95] feels so strongly about this matter that Webb encloses a letter from him.

Noah's letter to Webb asserts that the Farmers' and Mechanics' Bank will not allow any more banks to be chartered in Albany. Meanwhile, Albany is growing richer year by year. He has been assured that capital for a railroad from Utica to Schenectady has been set up. Every businessman of credit and capital will sign an application for a branch. The Albany merchants are *direct* importers. They do not get their supplies from New York City. Finally, a branch will intimidate the opposition.[96]

Despite all these persuasive arguments, Nicholas Biddle rejected the idea of opening a branch at Albany and wrote of his decision to both Devereaux at Utica and to Bloodgood in Al-

[93] Bray Hammond, *Banks and Politics in America* (Princeton: Princeton University Press, 1957), p. 393.
[94] Editor of the New York *Courier and Enquirer.*
[95] Coeditor of the *Courier and Enquirer* along with Webb.
[96] Webb to Biddle, November 30, 1831, NBP.

bany, on December 23rd [97] and December 26th respectively.[98] He also wrote Campbell P. White, then in Congress, that no decision *has as yet been made on a branch in Albany. White's recommendation of Mr. Stevenson will be put before the board, if the branch is established.*[99] Why Biddle should not have written to White that there would be no branch, as he had to the other two men, is puzzling, for it seems the Regency was as opposed to the branch then as it had once been in favor of it. White's position seems to have been contrary to the Regency's in both 1826 and 1831. Perhaps Campbell White was one of the New York City Democrats who opposed the Regency but was persuaded to vote against the Bank in 1832.

We come now to early January, 1832, just a few days before Biddle made up his mind to apply during the current session of Congress for renewal of the charter. On January 3rd Bloodgood wrote again as follows:

If you apply this winter, say we, then establish a Branch and we can materially aid you and not *increase* the opposition in the least, as that is at its height here . . . if you do nothing for Albany, the greatest part of the petitioners whose names you have will connect themselves with the local applications now pending. There is no mistake in this. You will lose the very best set of applicants, the best set of names ever sent you from this city. One of the firm of Fidler & Taylor called but a few days since on Mr. Campbell to know at once what was the prospect, as he was determined to wait no longer but connect himself with a local Bank which will most probably be chartered. So with the others. I wish I could impress this part of my subject upon you. In one word, you will not have a dozen of the applicants left you in the spring. It will be more than folly to establish a branch here without securing respectable, responsible and active business patrons. I have not therefore promulgated the contents of your letter to me,[100] as it would break us up.

[97] Biddle to Devereaux, December 23, 1831, PLB.
[98] Biddle to Bloodgood, December 26, 1831, PLB.
[99] Biddle to White, December 23, 1831, PLB.
[100] He must be referring to the letter Biddle wrote refusing the branch in Albany.

But other decisive circumstances have occurred since my last—viz.,

Mr. Livingston, *our* candidate for Speaker, has been elected by our assembly by a large majority over Mr. Olcott's candidate for whom there was a desperate drive in *vain*. Mr. Livingston is notoriously in favor of rechartering the United States Bank. The members generally understood this point and acted accordingly.

In addition, I have been to Troy and through some intelligent friends have ascertained that the leading Jacksonians of Troy are in favor of the United States Bank, that the ——[101] Editor can be brought out in favor of the recharter and the appointment of a couple of Directors for that town will be a most acceptable kindness. Mr. Campbell and myself were up last evening, and we have made arrangements to draw up a petition which we are assured will be signed by the warmest politicians in that city. This you may consider as done.

A new daily Jackson paper called the Craftsman has commenced its existence here today which has for its object the constraint of the unprincipled regency which has so long kept us in chains and the support of the United States Bank. His object will be to keep it up as long as the patronage he receives and the subscriptions we shall muster up for him will enable him.

Thus we are armed at all points and ready to do you essential service, if we are not whistled down the wind by your Bank. We offer you the best support, a certain and fair business, the friendship of Troy, Lansingburgh, ——,[102] and Schenectady, and the political aid of which you are in want. We tell you all this must be lost for many years unless enforced now and that the present feeling of disappointment will be succeeded by apathy, that here in this State and this city, the hardest part of your battle must be fought, and this position gained, all else is easy. . . .[103]

It thus becomes apparent that Biddle's decision not to establish the Albany branch either in 1826, when asked by the Regency to do so, or in 1832 was a very costly decision.

To emphasize this further, the following letter was written on the same day, January 3rd, from John Rathbone in Albany who

[101] The name of the newspaper is illegible.
[102] The name of this city is illegible.
[103] Bloodgood to Biddle, January 3, 1832, NBP.

was a director both of the Erie Railroad and of the New York City branch of the Bank. He addressed the letter to Isaac Lawrence, the president of the New York City branch:

The election of speaker in the House has weakened the influence of the Regency more than anything that has happened here in years—it turned on the United States Bank question; they brought that forward as the reason that C. L. Livingston should not be elected, and used all their arts to prevent it—it did not answer—the Western members had seen enough of the Western Branches to convince them that so far from answering the predictions of the ———[104] of the Van Buren regency, they had lowered interest from 7 to 6 per cent and afforded them accommodations they had never before experienced through Banks, and I am now fully convinced, had Mr. Biddle withheld the Buffalo Branch, and I think the Utica has done good, the Western part of this state would have nearly unanimously opposed the Institution, whereas, the Bank has now a powerful interest. . . .[105]

Rathbone was referring to that part of New York State that was shown in Chapter 1 to have voted solidly pro-Bank, and in miniature mirrored the behavior of the western part of the United States. Here we see again, as in the West, enthusiasm for the Bank among its legislators and its people.[106] Earlier it was mentioned [107] that New York State sent about forty citizens' memorials in favor of the Bank. Of these forty, about thirty came from the area west of the Hudson River. The people of the far West especially showed great fervor, the citizens of Niagara, Erie, Chatauqua, and Cattaraugus counties forwarding four joint memorials.[108]

However, unlike the national picture, the state banks of the

---

[104] One word is illegible.   [105] Rathbone to Lawrence, January 3, 1832, NBP.
[106] Both areas benefited economically from the Bank, but the far western part of New York State was involved in a political situation which provided additional motivation for its support. A detailed analysis of this involvement is being made at Columbia University by Neil Gold in a study of banks and politics in New York State during the Jackson period.
[107] See page 93, concerning the New York State memorials.
[108] These joint memorials have been counted as only four out of the forty, not as sixteen.

western sector gave the Bank no support, as will be reflected in the ensuing correspondence.

We come now, in point of time, to that very busy January 16th when Biddle wrote the bulk of his letters for petitions and memorials supporting renewal of the Bank's charter by the United States Congress. As usual, the tone of his letters to the three New York State branches indicates clearly the attitude of the state banks.

He wrote to Devereaux in Utica the usual opening paragraph as to Pennsylvania's action with respect to citizens' and state bank memorials. But he added: "I therefore wish to ask your advice about the propriety of any movement in your quarter. From the State Banks I presume no assistance could be expected, and it remains to consider the expediency of memorials from the citizens generally." [109]

To William B. Rochester, president of the Buffalo branch he writes: "Your State Banks would not I persume concur in it, but a memorial from the citizens generally without distinction of party, would be very acceptable." [110]

His hopes for New York City were not so negative, for he wrote Isaac Lawrence that it will be very desirable to obtain as universal an expression of public opinion on the subject as can be procured, and his purpose in writing now is to ask whether measures similar to those now in train here could not be adopted in New York State. Will Lawrence have the goodness to confer with the directors Messrs. Rathbone and Carow and such other friends as he may think it judicious to consult, and if practicable, put the measures in motion? [111] At the same time he asked Rathbone in Albany to get in touch with Lawrence.

On January 17th Isaac Lawrence answered to say that he, Rathbone, Lennox, Carow, and Saul Alley have met. Some state

[109] Biddle to Devereaux, January 16, 1832, PLB.
[110] Biddle to Rochester, January 16, 1832, PLB.
[111] Biddle to Lawrence, January 16, 1832, PLB.

banks will sign a memorial, others will not, though they may not oppose it. Mayor Bowne [112] has come out in favor of the Bank and will sign for it.[113]

Isaac Carow informed Biddle on the 19th:

I have conferred with Mr. Lawrence since the receipt of your favor of the 16th and have in consequence sounded several friends who are Directors of State Banks and the opinion generally expressed is that with the exception of the Manhattan and perhaps two other Banks, they could be induced to petition, but there will be a disposition to clog the petition with conditions such as subjecting the Bank to the State taxes, etc. I suggested to Mr. Lawrence that a copy of the Petition from the Philadelphia Banks would be useful to shew the grounds on which they placed their application and on which we wish it to be seconded. . . .[114]

Biddle forwarded the Pennsylvania State Bank memorial and asked Lawrence to get as many banks as he could to do the same.[115]

January 24th Lawrence acknowledges receipt and says that Mr. Alley and Mr. Rathbone have seen them. He expects Mr. Lennox any moment. He hopes tomorrow something will be done by the banks and the merchants. Then he adds a postscript saying that he has just seen Mr. Lennox and he thinks the presidents of principal banks will join in a memorial.[116]

So far, things seem to have been going nicely for the Bank. But signs of trouble developed the following day when William G. Buchnor, a Wall Street broker, wrote Biddle that Colt has sent him a copy of the memorial from the banks of Pennsylvania. Buchnor has talked to Mr. Catlin [117] and Mr. Wilkes. They concur in the statements made in the memorial, and are

---

[112] Democratic mayor of New York City at the time and known to have been pro-Bank.
[113] Lawrence to Biddle, January 17, 1832, NBP.
[114] Carow to Biddle, January 19, 1832, NBP.
[115] Biddle to Lawrence, January 23, 1832, PLB.
[116] Lawrence to Biddle, January 24, 1832, NBP.
[117] President of the Merchants Bank mentioned in the letter of 1826 from Campbell White—the bank which bent its will to the combination in control.

decidedly in favor of the renewal of the Bank on the most liberal terms. But, if this question is agitated now, because of so much opposition in the press from "our Banks and *individuals* connected with them," no memorial can be written on which a majority will agree. If the memorial should fail, Washington will interpret this as hostility to the Bank in New York City.[118]

Next, Robinson, the cashier of the New York City branch, lets Biddle know that Mr. Lennox has failed with the application to the banks for a memorial. Friends of the Bank are being urged not to do anything but to stay quiet. Robinson the day before asked Mr. M. D. Benjamin, a jobber on Pearl Street who has repeatedly urged Robinson to let him begin handing around a memorial for signatures, to begin a memorial. He instantly obtained 1,000 names. The Mayor would not put his name at the top, but John J. Astor did. Robinson adds that he never did like the application to banks. He feels generally they are hostile to the Bank.[119]

Isaac Lawrence followed up by saying that their hopes for the City banks to petition for renewal are at an end. Mr. Lennox is much disappointed, having calculated with great certainty that the principal part would agree to it. A petition is now circulating among the merchants "and will succeed *very satisfactorily*." [120]

For more details as to what transpired to alter the seemingly favorable position of the Bank, let us look at the letter Robert Lennox wrote on February 11th:

I have been urging with all the force in my power the ——[121] course you recommended, and which I thought was quite proper under the circumstances of the times and the position in which the Bank is placed by her applications to the Government. —It is a fact that some of our heaviest borrowers are Directors in the City Banks, and *said* to be hostile to their doing anything in aid of our charter. —I could name sources, but I suspect you know them—I have pressed the sub-

[118] Buchnor to Biddle, January 25, 1832, NBP.
[119] Robinson to Biddle, January 28, 1832, NBP.
[120] Lawrence to Biddle, January 30, 1832, NBP.   [121] One word is illegible.

ject on the Bank of New York till the President laid the matter before them—there was a great majority in favor of a memorial, but as the President wished unanimity, it was postponed till the minority had time to consider ——[122] are those I alluded to as heavy borrowers. —In the Manhattan, the President Mr. Gaston, Mr. Jergenson, Mr. Todd, Mr. Thomson and Mr. Kennedy are all friendly but they can do nothing against Mr. White [123] who is deadly and *now* openly hostile—I long thought so. . . .[124]

Where Lennox referred to state bank hostility as the *"said"* hostility, and underlined it for emphasis, there is the same implication that state bank hostility in New York City was something manufactured by its enemies, just as Biddle described it. Not any of the correspondence in response to Biddle's request for memorials, except for Robinson's statement, seems to support general massive hostility on the part of most of the directors and officers, but rather, it indicates a small but powerful and determined minority operating to further its own peculiar economic gains. Whether this group was linked closely with Olcott cannot be determined. But we do know that the combination of 1826 was said to control the City Bank, and we found that Olcott influenced the bank through his brother-in-law, Mr. North. Therefore, a connection may very well have existed.

There were several memorials signed by the merchants of New York City. The merchants state quite clearly the economic benefits they derive from the Bank. First, the branch notes of the Bank exchange in New York City either at par or at no less than one-fourth of one per cent below par. Second, whenever a pressure has existed in the money market, the Bank has helped the mercantile community. The merchants also assert that the rapid transfer of United States Bank stock has kept it from being a monopoly. The stock passes into currency. It passes from one

[122] The illegible words look like "this number of three" but one cannot be certain.
[123] Not Campbell P. White but Robert White according to the *New York Directory* for 1831–1832.
[124] Lennox to Biddle, February 11, 1832, NBP.

individual to another and back and forth between Europe and the United States in place of specie.[125]

Meanwhile, in response to Biddle's request to Devereaux in Utica for citizens' memorials, a letter arrived saying that the Regency is trying to get a resolution through the state legislature against renewal of the Bank's charter. Whether anything should be done in the area around Utica depends on the Regency's course.[126]

The following day Devereaux again wrote that his information as to what the friends of the Farmers' and Mechanics' Bank will do has caused him to go to Albany to counteract any resolution they might offer against the Bank. In the Senate that morning a resolution against the Bank was offered by one of them. The parties offering this were divided—but the friends of the Bank were firm. Could Biddle prevail upon one or two leading Jackson men in New York City to come there to Albany at this time to remonstrate with their friends and show to the moderate party men the views of the Jackson Party in the state of Pennsylvania? Much good will result from this.[127]

On the 27th of January Devereaux sent another letter saying that Mr. Olcott urged the resolution against the Bank and was surprised at the division among his friends. Many men go with Root, now in Congress, or with Livingston, now lieutenant-governor. Both are opposed "to what we call the Regency." The present resolution will pass the Senate but not the Assembly—at least, if it does it will be with so few more in favor than against so as to destroy the effects originally intended. He hopes the friends from New York City will arrive before it comes before the Assembly.[128]

Meanwhile Bloodgood warns Biddle again on January 28th:

[125] *Executive Documents*, 22nd Congress, 1st Session, vol. IV, doc. 119.
[126] Devereaux to Biddle, January 23, 1832, NBP.
[127] Devereaux to Biddle, January 26, 1832, NBP.
[128] Devereaux to Biddle, January 27, 1832, NBP.

I have every day persons connected with the application for a Branch here calling on me for information as to its present chances. I therefore must beg of you to let me know on receipt of this what those chances are. I regret exceedingly you did not close with our application at once, as we could have effectively put down the present Resolution which I fear will pass the Legislature. I have had several confidential communications with the Speaker Mr. Livingston [129] on the subject and I am at liberty to state some facts within his and my knowledge as to this business.

Although Mr. Livingston did not consider his election as indicative of the sentiments of the House, yet the regency opposed him on the ground of his being in favor of the recharter, and since that time they have by the usual course of things, personal solicitations and threats, management brought [*sic*] over a great number of those members who came here at first inclined to act independently. If there had been a respectable Direction with a branch here, we could have very properly taken pains to come out and produce a reaction. The more I see of this matter, the more I am convinced that our position is not sufficiently estimated. You cannot bring yourselves to believe that with the vast extent and the great power of your operations, a point like Albany should be the first on which your institution turns. And so it is and you will find it out in the end. Mr. Van Buren controls the *central power*, and that power controls the Legislature and a majority of the Counties. As Mr. Livingston says, "there is no resisting them—we are led like sheep to the slaughter." The moment a man refuses to do as he is told, that moment they put him down by the thousand ways in which, if a business man, his credit, or a politician, his character assailed.

The letter goes on to entreat Biddle to indicate that he will establish a branch in Albany. Just as Campbell P. White had recommended Stevenson as president should the Albany branch be established, so had Mr. Bloodgood, for he goes on to say that although he has favored Mr. Stevenson, he thinks the present president of the state bank would be willing to take the presidency of the branch Bank, and this would place it above any es-

[129] This was Charles Livingston; the lieutenant-governor was Edward Livingston.

tablishment in the area. Mr. Stevenson is about to be made president of the Firemen's Insurance Company: [130]

There is a great distress for money here just now. The best paper will not command it as our Banks have been using State funds for the last year or two, and as they now are obliged to hand them over to Banks willing to pay a higher rate for deposits, they are pressed to an unusual degree. A branch here would be of immense service, at this moment. . . . It would unite the business men who want money.[131]

The situation in Albany, with respect to the businessmen, seems to have been a very difficult one. Apparently, since Olcott controlled so many banks and at the same time would not allow any more banks to be chartered, he had forced the business community into dependence on him for loans. Consequently, they were compelled to remain silent. But if they had had a branch of the Bank to turn to, they would not have been afraid to unite in support of renewing its charter.

What of the state banks in the area? On February 15th Rathbone sent from Albany a memorial from "the most respectable citizens." He writes that he could have secured more names, but could not go back again because of lack of time. This is why a man such as Spencer [132] is not on the list. However, "the director of nearly all of our Banks is in . . .[133] and three of the Presi-

[130] Thomas Olcott at just this time was accused of refusing to discount the note of Mr. Simmons, described as a highly respectable and responsible business man in Albany, because Simmons would not sign a proxy giving Olcott the right to vote for a friend of Olcott's as a new director of the Firemen's Insurance Company. The *New York American* of February 13, 1832, reprints the accusation from the *Albany Daily Advertiser*. On February 15, 1832, the *New York American* published Olcott's letter of denial to the *Albany Argus*. The letter was carried in full because as the *New York American* says, ". . . a phrase omitted, or a tone changed, may account for both versions, and still leave the truth unascertained. We are content that Mr. Olcott's version should avail what it may avail." Olcott's letter admits asking Simmons for the proxy but denies that his refusal to sign had any connection with the refusal to discount the $5,000 note. Olcott claims he refused the note because Simmons wanted the money too quickly.
[131] Bloodgood to Biddle, January 28, 1832, NBP
[132] Probably John C. Spencer, New York State senator from the 8th District.
[133] Because of the errors in grammar here, it is hard to tell quite what was meant.

dents." Not over four or five who were asked refused. Rathbone
tells Biddle to forward the memorial to whom he pleases—Marcy
or Dudley will present it—or anyone he wishes.[134]

All we can deduce from this is that there did exist some state
banks in and around Albany that favored the Bank. We also
know that the State Bank of New York, located in Albany, sent
its own memorial and from Burroughs it appears that the Utica
Bank supported the United States Bank.

However, from all the other correspondence we are justified
in concluding that state bank hostility of the most violent sort
emanated from Albany, spreading itself from New York City to
Lockport in the northwestern part of the state and was so powerful that it was suspected of being the cause of the New York
resolution against the Bank. Even Biddle finally became convinced of this, for on February 25, 1832, he wrote George Dallas that he is absolutely certain the Farmers' and Mechanics'
Bank has caused the resolution against the Bank.[135] By this time
it was a little too late for Biddle to take the corrective measures
which he was urged so repeatedly to take.

To sum up each of the three influential regions of New York
State: The City representatives in the New York State Senate
and Assembly were pro-Bank, as, most probably were the majority of those who elected them. Several favorable memorials
were written up and signed by merchants from the City, and
there is no evidence suggesting anti-Bank sentiment among the
populace. As to the state banks in the City, there existed as early
as 1826 a group of people who held rather extensive control
over several banks and who wanted to control the Bank. The
only link mentioned between Thomas Olcott and this group was
his influence on the City Bank,[136] which was part of the association's holdings. There could not have been very open and ob-
vious hostility on the part of the New York City banks; other-

---

[134] Rathbone to Biddle, February 15, 1832, NBP.
[135] Biddle to Dallas, February 25, 1832, PLB.   [136] See Olcott, p. 101.

wise such a group of successful men as Robert Lennox, John Rathbone, Saul Alley, Isaac Lawrence, and Isaac Carow would have had some awareness of it when they first conferred and predicted that most City banks would sign a petition. Even after consulting many officers of these banks, they still felt assured of their opinion. Ultimately, however, no petitions were produced. Some hostility certainly existed, for the friends of the Bank were cautioned to "stay quiet." Once again fear of reprisal from the enemy points to the existence of antagonism. The correspondence suggests a hostile powerful minority at the root, some of whom, as in 1826, were heavy borrowers from the Bank.

The populace of the western part of New York State was as unequivocally friendly to the Bank as were its legislators. Rathbone's letter suggesting anti-Bank sentiment in this area prior to the establishment of the Buffalo and Utica branches in 1829 and 1830 is noteworthy here. After the people had experienced the benefits of the Bank through these branches, their attitude changed completely. The state banks of the western area, however, offered no support, just as Biddle had anticipated.

The political atmosphere of the Albany area was so complicated that it is hard for us to discern the truth. But it is fairly clear that the state legislature started out early in 1831 more favorably disposed toward the Bank than otherwise. However, *The legislature's* final action was a patently hostile one, as evidenced by its instructions to the New York State delegation in Congress to vote against the Bank. From Burroughs we know that the Genesee Bank was friendly to the United States Bank, and other correspondence mentions that a memorial was signed by the officers of the New York State Bank. Some officers of state banks also signed citizens' petitions. Side by side with this support was the strongest display of state bank hostility reflected in the entire correspondence. As to the people of the area, clearly the businessmen favored the Bank, but fear of Olcott inhibited overt action on their part, except for one memorial.

Overall, New York State must be counted by July of 1832 as a powerful enemy of the Bank. Not, however, because the majority of its people or state banks behaved with hostility, but because both the state legislature and the New York State representatives in Congress voted down the Second United States Bank, driven by the Regency and Olcott to do so.

8

Conclusion

OUR INQUIRY to determine the identity and extent of the support for the Second Bank of the United States has led us to a state by state analysis of the attitudes of the state banks, the national and state legislatures, and the populace in general. The investigation has been based in large part on material which ought to spell out with the greatest clarity, if any evidence can, the reasons why people supported or failed to support the Bank—that is, petitions to Congress. As we have seen, the Jacksonian politicians against the Bank were a well-organized group spreading a ·strong net of influence throughout the Union. Despite efforts from Washington, however, they were able to raise no state bank memorials against the Bank and only eight anti-Bank citizens' memorials. In contrast to this, the Bank's supporters forwarded to Congress 118 citizens' memorials and about seventy state bank memorials.

We have found that Nicholas Biddle was correct when he said, "state banks in the main are friendly." Specifically, only in Georgia, Connecticut, and New York was there positive evidence of hostility. A majority of state banks in some states of the South, such as North Carolina and Alabama, gave strong support to the Bank as did both the Southwest states of Louisiana and Mississippi. Since Virginia gave some support, we can claim that state banks in the South and Southwest for the most part supported the Bank. New England, contrary to expectations, showed the banks of Vermont and New Hampshire behind the Bank, but the support of Massachusetts was both qualitatively and quantitatively weak. The banks of the Middle states all supported the Second Bank except for those in New York. There, the Mechanics' and Farmers' Bank together with the other banks Olcott controlled "arrayed a powerful force against the Bank." Aside from Olcott's interests, the influence exerted against the Bank by the state banks was insignificant. In Connecticut, for example, several officers of banks along with a few citizens signed an anti-Bank memorial. But this was the extent of their effectiveness, for the Connecticut legislature voted unanimously for the Second Bank.

What can we conclude, in summary, about the attitude of the people in these different areas? Only a handful of anti-Bank memorials was signed, hence it is impossible to call the populace hostile. However, from the evidence of pro-Bank memorials it *is* possible to see that the most enthusiastic efforts to support the Bank came from the West. Actually, popular support for the Bank can be claimed for more areas than just the West. Writing a memorial and securing hundreds and sometimes thousands of names to it is a very positive act, requiring energy inspired by strong feeling. Especially was this the case with regard to the Second Bank. The popular President Jackson had come out against the Bank in his annual messages to Congress in 1829 and 1830, so his position with respect to the institution was well known to the people. What percentage of pro-Bank citizens would have had the courage to affix their names to memorials diametrically opposed to the views of their admired President? Yet about 118 pro-Bank memorials were recorded as having been presented to Congress. In contrast, even with the President behind them, only eight memorials against the Bank were organized and forwarded to Congress. The least, then, that we have a right to claim is that there was stronger pro-Bank than anti-Bank feeling among the people of the United States at that time. Furthermore, the geographic distribution of the supporting memorials was fairly widespread—New Hampshire, Vermont, Massachusetts, Connecticut, New York, Pennsylvania, Maryland, some southern states, and the West. New York was not represented solely by the merchants in the City and the citizens of the far western section. Albany, Herkimer, Jefferson, Otsego, and Oneida Counties, among others, sent in memorials.

Now we return to the question originally raised in Chapter 1: how could the "Bank War" have been waged so fiercely and for so long with just a tiny band of supporters consisting of stockholders of the Bank, its employees, and a few prominent statesmen confronting such a mighty array of the Bank's enemies? Actually we can claim that in 1832, at the most crucial period in the Bank's history, the Bank was supported by most state legislatures, by a majority in both Houses of the United States Congress, by an impressive number of state banks, and by more direct expressions of pro-Bank than anti-Bank feeling among the people at large.

But now we have succeeded only in reversing the question originally posed, for now a mighty array of supporters faces a small minority opposed to the Bank. Having placed ourselves in this awkward position we are bound to say something about the causes of the Bank's destruction. We cannot take refuge behind the agrarian people of the frontier areas or the numerous state banks. Can we perhaps blame the "eastern mechanic?" But we have Root's convincing statement in the New York Senate to the contrary, as well as several pro-Bank memorials from Massachusetts and Philadelphia signed specifically by mechanics. A Massachusetts memorial is captioned "Manufacturers and Mechanics," and one from Philadelphia reads specifically "Manufacturers, Mechanics, Merchants and Others." John Quitman, writing a letter from New York City where he was visiting in July, 1831, says that "the working interest" along with manufacturers and other groups inclined toward Clay and the American System.[1] The American System meant support of the Bank, high tariffs, and internal improvements.

[1] J. F. H. Claiborne, *Life and Correspondence of John A. Quitman* (2 vols., New York: Harper and Brothers, 1860), I, p. 108.

Was it the "business man's dislike of the federal Bank's re-
straints upon bank credit?" If so, we must read as meaningless
the eloquent pleas for a branch Bank in Albany to relieve the
distress of the businessman left in the hands of the state banks,
and ignore the countless number of businessmen's signatures on
memorials from New York City, Boston, Philadelphia, and elsewhere. We would also have to disregard the belief reflected in
many memorials that the agrarian, manufacturing, and other economic interests fluctuated together and were dependent in
common on the Bank for their expansion and well-being. Very
few business houses in New York City seem to have sided with
Jackson against the Bank.[2] Earlier we found that the merchants
in the City had volunteered to circulate a favorable petition and
as soon as permission was granted they secured 1,000 names
within twenty-four hours.

What, then, did destroy the Second Bank of the United
States?

The failure of Congress to recharter the Bank and the consequent destruction of the Bank has been implicit throughout this
investigation. Perhaps a more precise way to state this is to say
that the Bank was destroyed because Congress failed to raise a
two-thirds majority to override the Veto. It is to this problem,
then, that we must address ourselves. Realizing that there was a
majority in both Houses in favor of the Bank, even without
counting those Congressmen who voted against the Bank but
were really pro-Bank in sentiment, we must try to indicate why
the necessary majority could not be mustered.

It is important to understand that the decisive conflict over
the Bank was not only between the National Republicans and
the Democrats, as is so commonly thought, but was also within
the Democratic Party itself. The National Republicans were out-
and-out Bank supporters, but the Democratic Party embraced
substantial numbers of men on both sides of the Bank question.

[2] George Douglas was apparently one of the few. See Joseph Alfred Scoville,
Old Merchants of New York (New York: T. R. Knox, 1885), p. 38.

As has already been pointed out, those who voted against the Bank but were pro-Bank in sentiment cast their votes the way they did because they gave Jackson's reelection priority over the Bank issue. Had they cast their votes in favor of the Bank, the renewal of the charter would have been assured. But party unity came first. Now the idea of "Party first," although a widely recognized principle of political behavior, carries with it a certain opprobrium. The Van Buren and Biddle manuscripts and Niles' *Register*, however, provide impressive material which both explains and partly justifies the Jacksonian Democrats' adherence to this principle in 1832.

It will be recalled that Van Buren at that time was our minister to the Court of St. James in England, having been appointed to the post by Jackson after Van Buren had resigned as Secretary of State. In those days it was assumed that appointment to the office of Secretary of State indicated the President's choice of his future successor. Van Buren had discharged his duties as Secretary honorably, and the approval by the Senate of his appointment as minister to England should conventionally have passed that chamber. However, Calhoun, vice-president of the United States and presiding officer of the Senate, had been rejected in favor of Van Buren as Jackson's successor, and consequently viewed Van Buren as his political archenemy. The vote in the Senate was rigged, 26–26, so Calhoun could have the satisfaction of casting the deciding vote against Van Buren. It then became necessary to recall Van Buren after he had been representing this country for some time. This was an unusually petty act of vindictiveness on Calhoun's part, and it was sanctioned by Webster and Clay, already identified with the cause of the Bank.[3] With the tenuousness of England's respect for the United States, the full humiliation to the country as a whole—

---

[3] Niles' *Register* of February 25, 1832, quotes the *Richmond Enquirer* as referring to the rejection as "the prostration of the dignity and integrity of the Senate of the United States by the coalition of Clay, Calhoun and Webster."

but especially of President Jackson and Van Buren—can be imagined.[4] But seldom has an act been so fully revenged. Its repercussions can be seen from the following correspondence.

The day of the Senate vote, January 26, 1832, one of Biddle's lobbyists, Ingersoll, had just arrived in Washington. He wrote Biddle that day saying that the Speaker of the House, who was against the Bank, has nonetheless warned him that nothing is more likely to defeat the Bank issue than bad timing in the presentation of the petition for renewal of its charter.[5] Ingersoll goes on to tell Biddle of Van Buren's rejection and describes how various senators voted on the matter.[6]

Voluminous letters were written to Van Buren in England over this incident both by people politically sympathetic with him and by others who differed from him. Among these letters is one from Elijah Hawood, Washington, dated January 30th. He informs Van Buren of his rejection and says that it would have been impossible except for the influence of the Bank operating against him. Certain senators' votes could not have been procured without that influence.[7] But Hawood prophesies that this act will rebound: as a direct result of this,[8] Van Buren will first be vice-president, and then president. A letter from William Carroll of Nashville to Andrew Jackson says much the same as Hawood. Carroll explains that "two men know him, now, to one, that knew him sixty days ago." He adds that Van Buren

[4] Even Webster himself said that the rejection of the nomination would be regarded by foreign states as not favorable to the character of our government. See Niles' *Register*, February 4, 1832.

[5] George Dallas of Pennsylvania when presenting to the Senate the Bank's memorial for renewal of its charter remarked that he had discouraged presentation of the document at that time because "he felt deep solicitude and apprehension, lest, in the progress of the inquiry and in the development of views, under present circumstances it might be drawn into real or imagined conflict with some higher, some more favorite, some more immediate wish or purpose of the American people." See Niles' *Register*, January 9, 1832.

[6] Ingersoll to Biddle, January 26, 1832, NBP.

[7] There is no evidence in the Biddle manuscripts to support this statement.

[8] Hawood to Van Buren, January 30, 1832, Van Buren Manuscripts. Numerous letters predicted this same outcome.

will now be supported by the Jacksonians, whereas Calhoun's friends have all disappeared in the last ten days.[9]

From the Van Buren manuscripts we learn that on the same day Hawood's letter was written there was a special meeting called at Tammany Hall in New York City to protest the action of the Senate. Attendance at the meeting cut across both factions of the Democratic Party. A resolution against the Senate's action was signed both by members of the Regency and by others who, like Saul Alley, were not Regency members.[10]

Charles Butler of New York wrote on January 31st to Van Buren saying that the people have been roused against the vote, but that in the end all will be for his good. He tells Van Buren that the most respectable people were at the Tammany meeting.[11]

William A. Duer wrote to Colt, Biddle's close advisor, that he is ashamed of the Senate's behavior, even though he differs from Van Buren on many political matters.[12]

On February 4th Ingersoll again wrote Biddle from Washington about this incident. He says that he regrets Van Buren's rejection—this turns Jackson's men against everything that is supported by Webster and Clay, such as the Bank.[13] James Watson Webb, also in Washington to do what he could for the Bank, wrote Biddle a long letter appraising the congressional situation, in which he says much the same thing, adding that the rejection has drawn Jackson Party lines very tight.[14]

Because Webster and Clay symbolized pro-Bank sentiment, Van Buren's rejection had the effect both of unifying Regency and anti-Regency people within the Party and of turning some of them against the Bank.

[9] Carroll to Jackson, February 20, 1832, Papers of Andrew Jackson, vol. V, 2nd Series.
[10] January 30, 1832, Van Buren Manuscripts.
[11] Butler to Van Buren, January 31, 1832, Van Buren Manuscripts.
[12] Duer to Colt, January 31, 1832, Van Buren Manuscripts.
[13] Ingersoll to Biddle, February 4, 1832, NBP.
[14] Webb to Biddle, February 6, 1832, NBP

This incident in the Senate is not new to any historian, though the intensity of feeling it aroused, with consequent repercussions on both the Democratic Party and the Bank, has perhaps not been fully appreciated. Niles' *Weekly Register* from January through March of 1832 reflects the relative importance of the issue. Almost every publication refers to the matter giving it prominence as the first or second article on the first page or reporting at great length the Senate debates on the question.[15] The incident further corroborates Marvin Meyers' contention that the "Bank War" forged and gave character to the Jacksonian Party.[16] Actually the effect of the incident was to provide a rationale for the principle of "Party first." It was also another dramatic step towards turning the Bank question, not primarily a political issue, into a matter of party politics. Obviously the whole burden of Congress' failure to override the veto cannot be attributed to the rejection of Van Buren. But it could hardly have failed to influence some of the wavering pro-Bank Democrats. It is interesting to notice that eight of the nine senators referred to earlier [17] as having voted against the Bank but believed to be pro-Bank in sentiment voted for Van Buren's confirmation.[18]

Earlier, when Virginia was under consideration, discussion of additional correspondence from that state was postponed until the rest of the country had been examined. Since these letters offer evidence bearing on the present investigation, now is the appropriate point at which to consider them. On June 14, 1830, Henry Clay wrote to Biddle:

Unless I am deceived by information, received from one of the most intelligent Citizens of Virginia, the plan was laid at Richmond during a visit made to that place by the Secretary of State [19] last autumn, to make the destruction of the Bank the basis of the next Presidential

[15] See especially Niles' *Register* of January 21st and 28th, February 4th, 11th, 18th, 25th, and March 17th, 1832.
[16] See Meyer's contention, p. 3.   [17] See the senate vote, pp. 15–16.
[18] Niles' *Register*, February 4, 1832.   [19] Martin Van Buren.

Election. The message of the President, and other indications, are supposed consequences of that plan.[20]

According to McGrane, Van Buren was known to have been in Richmond in the fall of 1829. "Therefore," he suggested, "the question arises, could the Southern politicians have induced or suggested to Van Buren the idea of an attack on the Bank, holding out to the latter the hope of the next Presidential election, while their main idea was to gain time for their own propaganda?" [21]

J. Robertson wrote Biddle from Virginia about a year later:

You must be very sensible of the deep rooted hostility among the prominent politicians in this State against the Bank of the United States. Every art and device has been employed by them, to infuse into the minds and keep alive, a similar feeling among the people— not by any discussions about the merits of the Bank, or about its constitutionality, but by starting such topics, and repeating such charges and insinuations against the Institution and its management, as are calculated to strengthen and even inflame the prejudices of their adherents. In this work of delusion and mischief, you have probably seen, the *Richmond Enquirer* take the lead. Besides the Editor's own disingenous [sic] and deceptive observations, he is continually endorsing and dealing out to his readers, the slanderous and calumnious paragraphs and statements of such profligate presses throughout the Union, as are embarked in the same cause. And yet the truth is, he knows nothing about the Bank, or about Banking, and he cares nothing about them. . . . In seeming to attach so much importance to what is said in the *Enquirer* about the Bank, I may as well add, that I have good reasons for believing, that its course is approved of in Washington. And I have also equally good reasons for believing, that it is the course which was marked out eighteen months ago to be pursued in certain contingencies.[22]

We have admittedly stressed that the Jacksonians did not want the Bank raised as an issue before the election. But the

---

[20] Reginald C. McGrane ed., *Correspondence of Nicholas Biddle* (Boston: Houghton Mifflin Company, 1919), p. 105.
[21] *Ibid.*, p. 105.   [22] Robertson to Biddle, July 4, 1831, NBP.

above evidence does not contradict this; it is chronology that has entered to confuse us. We have claimed that in *1832* they did not want the issue raised. In the fall of 1829 it was not yet apparent to the politicians how the Bank was gaining in popular favor. To support this point of view, there is a letter from Degrand in Boston dated April 5, 1831, which asks of Biddle: "Shall we also triumph in New York? Is Van Buren frightened at his attack on the Bank?—Has he *now* become aware of its increased and increasing popularity?" [23]

But all that need concern us now is that Virginia and New York were in some sense in league. Indeed, we need not even suppose them to be consciously in league to establish the point that both Virginia and New York were against the Bank and cast their votes that way. The four powerful states at this period, both with respect to the number of Congressional votes and in terms of influence, were New York, Pennsylvania, Massachusetts, and Virginia. It is apparent that both New York and Virginia were working very hard to gain support for their anti-Bank position. Olcott and the Regency, together with the Virginia politicians and the Virginia press, were making their position felt. So was Pennsylvania, as we have seen, but on the opposite side. How significant Massachusetts' apathy now becomes! Pennsylvania and the Bank needed rousing enthusiasm from Massachusetts. To counteract the impact of the Virginia–New York combination, it was important for Massachusetts not simply to vote in favor of the Bank, but also to bombard Congress with as many memorials from state banks, citizens, and the state legislature, as could be mustered. Had Massachusetts brought such pressure to bear, undoubtedly this would at least have influenced some of the borderline members in Congress.

New York, and especially the Farmers' and Mechanics' Bank, must, however, bear the brunt of the responsibility. When we realize that a two-thirds majority consisted of 32 votes in the

[23] Degrand to Biddle, April 5, 1831. NBP.

Senate and about 128 in the House of which the Bank was assured of 28 and 107 respectively, we see that the New York delegation, with two senators' and nineteen representatives' anti-
Bank votes, could almost by itself have swung the needed majority. Ironically enough, had the bill passed both Houses with a
somewhat larger majority than it did, there might very well
have been no need for an overriding two-thirds majority, for
there might not then have been a Veto. There are several letters
indicating that Jackson had changed his position regarding the
action he would take on the Bank bill. Charles F. Mercer, a congressman from Virginia, wrote Biddle on January 27, 1832, that
Mr. B.[24] of Tennessee has told him he will vote for renewal of
the Bank's charter.[25] But he also has told him that unless the
Bank bill passes by a considerable majority, General Jackson will
not approve it. He goes on to tell Mercer that Jackson has said
that he has twice stated his objections to renewal. But if the people sustain the Bank by a large majority, so will he.[26] Secretary
Livingston and Ingersoll met on February 27th and Livingston
asked Ingersoll to find out from Biddle whether he will agree to
the President's terms for a new charter.[27] Biddle accepts the
terms.[28] When Ingersoll reported this to Livingston, Livingston
said, "If such a bill goes to him as he can sign, he will sign it
without hesitation." [29]

Thomas Payne Govan, however, rejected the theory that
Jackson wavered. His rejection was based on an undated memorandum in Jackson's handwriting which Govan believed was
written in January, 1832. The memorandum referred to the
Bank as unconstitutional and said that if one is necessary, it must
have no concern with corporations.[30]

[24] John Bell, a representative in Congress from Tennessee.
[25] He ultimately voted against the Bank.
[26] Mercer to Biddle, January 27, 1832, NBP.
[27] Ingersoll to Biddle, February 23, 1832, NBP.
[28] Biddle to Ingersoll, February 25, 1832, NBP.
[29] Ingersoll to Biddle, March 1, 1832, NBP.
[30] Thomas P. Govan, *Nicholas Biddle, Nationalist and Public Banker, 1786–1844*
(Chicago: University of Chicago Press, 1959), p. 184.

Thomas Olcott's role is especially significant when we recall that the New York legislature was sufficiently pro-Bank at the time Morehouse first tried to obtain a vote on his resolution against renewal of the Bank's charter to shelve the issue. But Olcott's determined pressure, supported by the Regency, was effective enough first to move a pro-Bank majority to a tie of 55–55 and then to reduce it to an anti-Bank vote of 73–35.

But, if we place some of the responsibility on Olcott, then Nicholas Biddle must also shoulder his share. For he, with the immense power of the United States Bank behind him, was in a position to take a decisive step in Albany which was probably the only means of curtailing Olcott's influence. From 1826 on he had been made aware of Albany's economic needs, and later was specifically cautioned as to the weight of the Farmers' and Mechanics' influence. But he chose not to act. Perhaps to a resident of the important city of Philadelphia it appeared impossible for Albany to play such a pivotal role. As Biddle was forewarned, however, he "found it out in the end."

These are just some of the reasons, for surely there are more, as to why the Veto could not be overriden. Since it was not the intention of the present undertaking to attempt to explain the demise of the Bank but only to discover its supporters, no further exploration in the direction of the former topic will be attempted. Yet one further comment might be ventured.

Superficially it may appear that once again, in explaining the destruction of the Bank, we have been caught in the political trap. This is only partially true. Actually both politics and economics were involved. The rejection of Van Buren was indeed political. Massachusetts' apathy was not. Rather, it existed as a result of that state's relative economic independence. This was true also of Virginia, New York, and Connecticut, for they all had admirable banking systems of their own.

Likewise, those areas most vocal in support of the Bank were primarily motivated by economic dependence on the Bank, lacking both capital and a circulating medium of their own. The "economic motives" of Thomas Olcott have already been discussed.

It is still of interest to ask how the theory of nation wide state bank hostility gained such a strong foothold in men's minds. Anyone writing on the Jacksonian era is likely to read Jabez Hammond's *Political History of New York*. This book is a gold mine of information about the period, Hammond having been an informed contemporary of many prominent men of his day. About 1820 he was a member of the New York Senate from Cherry Valley, Otsego County. It will be remembered that Olcott had control of the banking in Cherry Valley. In addition, Morehouse, who presented the resolution against the Bank in the New York Assembly, was an agent of the Olcott group. Interestingly enough, he too came from Otsego County. Hammond, therefore, was fully exposed to the state banks' hostility and politicking, for he lived in their midst, and Olcott was said to have dealt not just secretly but also openly to gain his ends. It might not be wrong to suggest that Jabez Hammond may have attributed to the nation at large what he saw locally. This is not too far-fetched, given the poor transportation and communication of those days. Men often had to reason from their particular situation to a generalization about distant parts which they had not experienced firsthand. For instance he said, "Was it in human nature, and especially, was it in *bank nature*, . . . to resist this prospect of adding to their gains?"

We found in our investigation that banks could and did resist immediate short-run gains in favor of long-run ones. A comment on this problem is made in the letter from Robinson of Virginia to Biddle, in which he tells Biddle of Girard's statement that as a *banker* he will be better off if the Bank is not rechartered, but not as a merchant.[31] Robinson expresses suprise at Girard's making such a foolish statement. He adds that Girard surely must see that if the demise of the Bank brings in its wake the

[31] See Robinson's letter, p. 92.

calamities Girard claims it will, then *both* as a banker and a merchant he will be worse off.

Catterall carried the state bank hostility theory one step further and claimed that the United States Bank had been particularly offensive to the banks of the South and West, and consequently the Bank could count on opposition from most of these corporations.[32] He was quite correct in saying that the Bank had hurt this area badly, but such behavior dated back to the very early years of the Bank. Meanwhile Biddle's generous attitude in later years toward the South and West had altered opinions. But from such statements it can be understood why the theory of widespread state bank opposition came to be so generally accepted by historians.

Another interesting question which we might consider is why the people of the West should have come to be singled out as representing the heart of anti-Bank sentiment. Because the Bank was made a political issue in the election of 1832, some writers have concluded that a vote for Jackson meant a vote against the Bank, and have believed that those areas giving Jackson the heaviest support were the most anti-Bank states. The West, except for Clay's state, Kentucky, greatly favored Jackson. Indeed, Van Buren in his *Autobiography*, a book naturally included in the bibliographies of most writers on the Bank, said of the election results: "The will of the people in regard to the bank had been most clearly expressed on its own appeal and according to the forms of the constitution." [33] Even Andrew Jackson said on September 18, 1833, in a cabinet communication: "Can it now be said that the question of a recharter of the Bank was not decided at the election which ensued? [34]

---

[32] Ralph C. H. Catterall, *The Second Bank of the United States* (Chicago: University of Chicago Press, 1903), p. 166.

[33] Martin Van Buren, *Autobiography*, ed. by John C. Fitzpatrick, Annual Report of the American Historical Association for the Year 1918 (2 vols., Washington: United States Government Printing Office, 1920), II, p. 627.

[34] T. F. Gordon, *The War on the Bank of the United States* (Philadelphia: Key and Biddle, 1834), p. 111.

There were some very convincing statements made in the United States Senate and House, however, contradicting Jackson and Van Buren. Henry Clay, speaking in the Senate and referring to the presidential campaign of 1832 remarked:

In the canvass which ensued, it was boldly asserted, by the partisans of the President, that he was not opposed to a Bank of the United States. . . . They maintained, at least wherever those friendly to a National Bank were in the majority, that his re-election would be followed by a recharter of the Bank with proper amendments . . . ; but they, nevertheless, contended, that these objections would be cured, if he was re-elected, and the Bank sustained. I appeal to the whole Senate, to my colleague, to the people of Kentucky, and especially, to the citizens of the city of Louisville, for the correctness of this statement.[35]

William Wilkins, senator from Pennsylvania, referring to the election of President Jackson addressed the Senate thus: "I do not think that result turned upon the question of the recharter of the Bank; nor was it a popular decision of that inquiry. . . . Thousands of voters threw their weight on the side of the successful candidate, who would vote for a National Bank tomorrow." [36]

In the House of Representatives, Moore of Virginia said:

Every gentleman here knows that Jackson would have been elected whether he was for or against the Bank. . . . The chartering of the Bank was not the only question upon which the Presidential election turned; on the contrary, it is probable that more than one half of those who voted for the present Chief Magistrate were, at that time, in favor of rechartering the Bank.[37]

Representative Wise of Virginia exclaimed in the House: "I, for one, once did think that the President would sanction such a charter. . . . On all proper occasions when using my feeble efforts to elect him, I confidently declared this belief to many of the people whom I represent." [38]

[35] *Ibid.*, p. 113.　　　[36] *Ibid.*, p. 114.　　　[37] *Ibid.*, p. 114.　　　[38] *Ibid.*, p. 114.

In a speech to the House Representative Chilton Allen remarked:

I deny that the election of General Jackson either proves or conduces to prove, that the people of the United States are opposed to a National Bank. General Jackson certainly went before the people, at the last election, as a Bank man. . . . Then, Sir, I undertake to say that the Jackson party, in every county and district in the United States, presented General Jackson to the people, . . . as friendly to a United States Bank, properly modified.[39]

Finally, John Quincy Adams argued for the same point of view. He referred to the House vote of June, 1832, on the Bank in which 107 voted in favor of rechartering and 85 against.[40] He pointed out that of those standing for reelection who had participated in this vote, the people returned those representatives in exactly the same proportions as they had voted in 1832, i.e., 51 of the 107 and 41 of the 85. This he found more truly reflected the people's attitude toward the Bank.[41]

We have also seen repeatedly in the Biddle correspondence that many people were pro-Bank but gave Jackson's reelection priority over the Bank. Further, it is quite clear that Jackson was reelected mainly because of his immense personal popularity. Bassett quoted Van Buren as saying that nothing but Jackson's popularity could have carried the people in the contest against the strongly entrenched Bank.[42] John Quincy Adams believed that Jackson's whole strength rested on his personal popularity founded on his military services.[43] On February 6, 1832, James Watson Webb wrote Biddle that he is convinced of the folly of Jackson's friends trying to postpone the Bank question until the following session. Whether Jackson signs or not, Webb declares,

[39] Ibid., p. 115. [40] The vote analyzed on Map 1, p. 8.
[41] Gordon, p. 116.
[42] John S. Bassett, The Life of Andrew Jackson (2 vols., New York: Doubleday, Page and Company, 1911), II, 650.
[43] John Quincy Adams, Memoirs of John Quincy Adams, ed. by Charles Francis Adams (Philadelphia: J. B. Lippincott & Co., 1874–1877).

it will not produce the slightest change in the prospect of his re-election.[44]

Chilton Allen stated about Jackson: "For the fact is, that his popularity was so overshadowing, that he could have been elected on any side of any question." [45]

These many opinions strongly emphasize that the question before the American people as they saw it was not whether they were voting for or against the Bank, but simply for or against Jackson who was represented to many of them as favoring a modified national bank.

As was suggested earlier, another factor contributing to the isolation of the Southwest and West as especially hostile areas was Catterall's error in analyzing only the Senate vote of 1832, the results of which supported his thesis. The impact of his opinion is heightened by his having singled out this area not just once with respect to the people as a whole, but a second time with respect to the state banks.

One of the most significant reasons for the disparity between the conclusions herein reached and those of many earlier writers concerns the period of the Bank's history under consideration. Most writers have chosen to explain the forces that destroyed the Second Bank by examining the whole span of twenty years during which the Bank was in existence. Wherever substantial hostility was observed, regardless of the year in which it occurred, it was charged with the responsibility of destroying the Bank. There has been a failure to distinguish between the long and short run. The present study has been an intensive one of the very short period just prior to the Veto of 1832, because this period seemed the most relevant to the problem at hand. The intriguing aspect of the Bank issue concerns events which occurred after the Bank had begun to function properly and the people had had the opportunity of experiencing its benefits. For only after this did the contradiction arise between its great service to the American

⁴⁴ Webb to Biddle, February 6, 1832, NBP.   ⁴⁵ Gordon, p. 115.

people and its demise. Before this period the situation was fairly easy to understand. Bad management under Jones, stringent management under Cheves, and the early years of growing mastery of the problem under Biddle led many groups to complain and express hostility toward the institution. That this was their attitude is fully understandable and natural, but not a very challenging situation to interpret. Neither those groups of people whose criticisms were directed at the Bank during its early or middle years, nor events of that period should necessarily be blamed for the Bank's destruction. The time was not yet ripe to judge. Not until the years chosen within the close compass of those discussed herein, after the Bank had matured and been experienced sufficiently long for its effects to be discernible, is it possible to identify those elements which led to its destruction.

Bibliography

I. MANUSCRIPTS

Papers of Nicholas Biddle. Washington, D.C.: Library of Congress, 1915.

Papers of Andrew Jackson. Washington, D.C.: Library of Congress, 1913.

Papers of Martin Van Buren. Washington, D.C.: Library of Congress, 1911.

II. PUBLIC DOCUMENTS

Acts of the General Assembly of the State of Georgia. October, November, and December, 1830.

Acts of the General Assembly of the State of Georgia. November and December, 1832.

Assembly Journal of New York State. 1831.

Journal of the Proceedings of the Legislative Council of the State of New Jersey, 1831.

Journal of the Proceedings of the Legislative Council of the State of New Jersey. 1832.

Journal of the Senate of the State of Delaware. 1832.

Laws of the State of Delaware. vol. 8.

Laws of the State of Indiana Passed and Published at the 14th Session of the General Assembly.

Laws of the State of Missouri Passed at the First Session of the Seventh General Assembly.

Missouri Statutes and Laws. 7, 1832.

New Jersey Journal of the General Assembly [Votes and Proceedings], 56th General Assembly of the State of New Jersey.

Senate Journal of New York State. 1831.

U.S. *Abridgement of the Debates of Congress.* vol. XI.

U.S. *Executive Documents,* 22nd Congress, 1st Session. vols. IV, VI.

U.S. *House Journal,* 22nd Congress, 1st Session.

U.S. *Register of Debates in Congress.* vol. VIII.

U.S. *Senate Documents,* 22nd Congress, 1st Session. vols. I, II.
U.S. *Senate Documents,* 23rd Congress, 2nd Session. vol. II.
U.S. *Senate Journal,* 22nd Congress, 1st Session.

III. NEWSPAPERS

Badger's *Weekly Messenger.* January–May, 1832.
New York American. January–June, 1832.
New York American Advocate. January, 1832.
New York Whig. January–June, 1832.
Niles' *Weekly Register.* January–July, 1832.

IV. MEMOIRS AND PRINTED CORRESPONDENCE

Adams, John Quincy. *Memoirs of John Quincy Adams.* Edited by
  Charles Francis Adams. 12 vols. Philadelphia: J. B. Lippincott and
  Company, 1874–1877. [VII–IX]
Barker, Jacob. *Incidents in the Life of Jacob Barker, of New Or-
  leans, Louisiana.* Washington: 1855.
Bennett, James Gordon. *Memoirs of James Gordon Bennett and His
  Times, by a Journalist.* New York: Stringer and Townsend, 1855.
Biddle, Nicholas. *Correspondence of Nicholas Biddle.* Edited by
  Reginald C. McGrane. Boston: Houghton Mifflin Company,
  1919.
Claiborne, John Francis Hamtramck. *Life and Correspondence of
  John A. Quitman.* 2 vols. New York: Harper and Brothers, 1860.
Fowler, John. *Journey of a Tour in the State of New York, in the
  Year 1830.* London: Whittaker, Treacher and Arnot, 1831.
Hamilton, James Alexander. *Reminiscences of James A. Hamilton.*
  New York: C. Scribner and Company, 1869.
Haswel, Charles Haynes. *Reminiscences of an Octogenarian of the
  City of New York, (1816–1860).* New York: Harper and Brothers,
  1896.
Hillard, George Stillman. *Memoir and Correspondence of Jeramiah
  Mason.* Cambridge: Riverside Press, 1873.
Hone, Philip. *The Diary of Philip Hone 1828–1851.* Edited by Allan
  Nevins. New York: Dodd, Mead & Company, 1927.
Kendall, Amos. *Autobiography of Amos Kendall.* Edited by Wil-
  liam Stickney. New York: P. Smith, 1949.

Tyler, Samuel. *Memoir of Roger Brooke Taney, LL.D., Chief Justice of the Supreme Court of the United States.* Baltimore: J. Murphy and Company, 1872.

Weed, Thurlow. *Life of Thurlow Weed.* Boston, New York: Houghton Mifflin and Company, 1884.

V. SECONDARY MATERIALS: BOOKS, ARTICLES, ETC.

Bassett, John Spencer. *The Life of Andrew Jackson.* 2 vols. New York: Doubleday, Page and Company, 1911.

Beach, Moses Yale. *The Wealth and Biography of the Wealthy Citizens of the City of New York.* New York: Sun Office, 1846.

Beard, Charles Austin. *Economic Origins of Jeffersonian Democracy.* New York: Macmillan Company, 1952.

Benson, Lee. *The Concept of Jacksonian Democracy; New York as a Test Case.* Princeton: Princeton University Press, 1961.

Biographical Dictionary of the American Congress 1774–1961. United States Government Printing Office, 1961.

Bradford, T. G. *Illustrated Atlas of the United States.* Boston: Weeks, Jordan and Company, 1838.

Brewer, Willis. *Alabama: Her History, Resources, War Record and Public Men From 1540–1872.* Montgomery: Barrett and Brown, 1872.

Brown, Henry. *A Narrative of the Anti-Masonic Excitement in the Western Part of the State of New York.* Batavia: Adams and M'Cleary, 1829.

Buell, Augustus C. *History of Andrew Jackson, Pioneer, Patriot, Soldier, Politician, President.* 2 vols. New York: Scribner's Sons, 1904.

Brown, Kenneth L. "Stephen Girard, Promoter of the Second Bank of the United States," *The Journal of Economic History,* II (November, 1942), 125–48.

Burr, David H. *Atlas of the State of New York.* New York: David H. Burr, 1829.

Byrdsall, F. *The History of the Loco-foco, or Equal Rights Party.* New York: Clement and Packard, 1842.

Catterall, Ralph C. H. *The Second Bank of the United States.* Chicago: University of Chicago Press, 1903.

Chaddock, Robert Emmet. *The Safety Fund Banking System in New*

York 1829–1866. Washington: United States Government Printing Office, 1910.

Chambers, William N. *Old Bullion Benton*. Boston: Little, Brown, 1956.

Claiborne, John Francis Hamtramck. *Mississippi as a Province, Territory and State*. vol. 1. Jackson: Power and Barksdale, 1880.

Clarke, Mathew St. Clair and Hall, D. A. *Legislative and Documentary History of the Bank of the United States*. Washington: Gales and Seaton, 1832.

Cole, Arthur Charles. *The Whig Party in the South*. Washington: American Historical Association, 1913.

Colton, Calvin. *The Life of Henry Clay, the Great American Statesman*. New York: Barnes, 1855.

Cross, Whitney R. *The Burned-over District*. Ithaca: Cornell University Press, 1950.

Dewey, Davis Rich. *Financial History of the United States*. New York: Longmans, Green and Company, 1903.

Disturnell, John. *A Gazetteer of the State of New York*. Albany: J. Disturnell, 1842.

Dodd, William Edward. *Expansion and Conflict*. Boston, New York: Houghton Mifflin Company, 1919.

Dorfman, Joseph. *The Economic Mind in American Civilization*. 5 vols. New York: Viking Press, 1946–59.

Eaton, Clement. *Henry Clay and the Art of American Politics*. Boston: Little, Brown, 1957.

Ellis, David Maldwyn, Frost, James A., Syrett, Harold C., and Carman, Harry J. *A Short History of New York*. Ithaca: Cornell University Press, 1957.

Fuess, Claude Moore. *Daniel Webster*. 2 vols. Boston: Little, Brown and Company, 1930.

Gallatin, Albert. *The Writings of Albert Gallatin*. Edited by Henry Adams. Philadelphia: J. B. Lippincott and Company, 1879.

Gammon, Samuel Rhea. *Presidential Campaign of 1832*. Baltimore: Johns Hopkins Press, 1922.

Golembe, Carter H. *State Banks and the Economic Development of the West 1830–44*. Doctoral Dissertation, Faculty of Political Science, Columbia University, New York, 1952.

Gordon, T. F. *The War on the Bank of the United States*. Philadelphia: Key and Biddle, 1834.

Gouge, William M. *A Short History of Paper Money and Banking in the United States.* Philadelphia: T. W. Ustick, 1833.

Govan, Thomas Payne. *Nicholas Biddle, Nationalist and Public Banker, 1786–1844.* Chicago: University of Chicago Press, 1959.

Hammond, Bray. *Banks and Politics in America.* Princeton: Princeton University Press, 1957.

————. "Jackson, Biddle and the Bank of the United States," *Journal of Economic History,* VII (May, 1947), 1–23.

————. "Public Policy and National Banks," *Journal of Economic History,* VI (May, 1946), 79–86.

————. "Long and Short Term Credit in Early American Banking," *The Quarterly Journal of Economics,* XLIX (November, 1934–August, 1935), 79–103.

Hammond, Jabez Delano. *The History of Political Parties in the State of New York.* 2 vols. New York: H. and E. Phinney, 1846.

Heath, Milton Sydney. *Constructive Liberalism.* Boston: Harvard University Press, 1954.

Herring, James. *National Portrait Gallery of Distinguished Americans.* 4 vols. Philadelphia: D. Rice and A. N. Hart, 1854.

Higgins, Ruth Loving. *Expansion in New York.* Columbus: Ohio State University, 1931.

Holdsworth, John Thom and Dewey, Davis R. *The First and Second Banks of the United States.* Washington: Government Printing Office, 1910.

Hough, Franklin B. *New York Civil List.* Albany: Weed, Parsons and Company, 1851.

Hunt, Charles Havens. *Life of Edward Livingston.* New York: D. Appleton and Company, 1864.

Hunt, Freeman. *Lives of American Merchants.* 2 vols. New York: Derby and Jackson, 1856.

Huntington, Charles Clifford. *A History of Banking and Currency in Ohio Before the Civil War.* Columbus: F. J. Heer Printing Company, 1915.

Jordon, Weymouth Tyrel, *The Public Career of George Washington Campbell.* Knoxville, 1938.

July, Robert William. *The Essential New Yorker.* Durham: Duke University Press, 1951.

Knox, John J. *A History of Banking in the United States.* New York: B. Rhodes and Company, 1900.

MacDonald, Grace E. *Check-list of Legislative Journals of the States of the United States of America*. Providence. Oxford Press, 1938.

MacKenzie, William Lyon. *Lives and Opinions of Benjamin F. Butler*. Boston: Cook, 1845.

———. *The Life and Times of Martin Van Buren*. Boston: Cook, 1846.

Mather, Joseph H. and Brockett, Linus Pierpont. *A Geographical History of the State of New York*. Utica: Fuller and Company, 1853.

McCarthy, Charles. *The Anti-Masonic Party*. American Historical Association Annual Report 1902. vol. I. Washington, 1903.

McNall, Neil Adams. *An Agricultural History of the Genesee Valley, 1790–1860*. Philadelphia: University of Pennsylvania Press, 1952.

Meigs, William Montgomery. *The Life of Charles Jared Ingersoll*. Philadelphia: J. B. Lippincott Company, 1897.

Memorial Record of Alabama. "Finances and Banking." Thomas H. Clark. 2 vols. Madison, Wisconsin: Brant and Fuller, 1893.

Meyers, Marvin. *The Jacksonian Persuasion: Politics and Belief*. Stanford: Stanford University Press, 1957.

Morgan, Forrest. *Connecticut as a Colony and as a State*. Hartford: The Publishing Society of Connecticut, 1904.

Parks, Joseph Howard. *Felix Grundy, Champion of Democracy*. University, Louisiana: Louisiana State University Press, 1940.

Parton, James. *Life of Andrew Jackson*. 3 vols. New York: Mason Bros., 1861.

Raguet, Condy. *A Treatise on Currency and Banking*. Philadelphia: Grigg and Elliott, 1840.

Redlich, Fritz. *History of American Business Leaders*. vol. 2. The Molding of American Banking, Men and Ideas. Ann Arbor: Edwards Brothers, Incorporated, 1940.

Remini, Robert Vincent. *Martin Van Buren and the Making of the Democratic Party*. New York: Columbia University Press, 1959.

Report of the Union Committee, New York, 1834. New York: Harper and Brothers, 1834.

Royall, William L. *Andrew Jackson and the Bank of the United States*. New York: G. P. Putnam's Sons, 1880.

Schlesinger, Arthur M., Jr. *Age of Jackson*. Boston: Little, Brown and Company, 1950.

Scoville, Joseph Alfred. *Old Merchants of New York*. New York: T. R. Knox, 1885.

Smith, H. Perry. *History of Buffalo and Erie County*. Syracuse: D. Mason and Company, 1884.

Smith, Walter B. *Economic Aspects of the Second Bank of the United States*. Cambridge: Harvard University Press, 1953.

Sowers, Don Conger. *Financial History of New York State*. PhD. Thesis, Columbia University, New York, 1914.

Sumner, William G. *Andrew Jackson*. Boston and New York: Houghton Mifflin, 1899.

Swisher, Carl Brent. *Roger B. Taney*. New York: Macmillan Company, 1935.

Turner, Fredrick J. *The United States, 1830–50; the Nation and Its Sections*. New York: H. Holt and Company, 1935.

Van Buren, Martin. *The Autobiography of Martin Van Buren*. Edited by John C. Fitzpatrick. 2 vols. Washington: United States Government Printing Office, 1920.

Van Deusen, G. G. *The Jacksonian Era*. New York: Harper Brothers, 1959.

Walters, Raymond, Jr. "The Origins of the Second Bank of the United States," *The Journal of Political Economy*, LIII (March–December, 1945), 115–131.

Weisenburger, Francis P. and Roseboom, Eugene H. *A history of Ohio*. Columbus: Ohio State Archaeological Society, 1953.

Werner, Morris Robert. *Tammany Hall*. Garden City: Doubleday Doran and Company, Inc., 1928.

Wettereau, James O. "The Branches of the First Bank of the United States," *Journal of Economic History* (Supplement, December, 1942), 66–100.

White, Leonard D. *The Jacksonians, A Study in Administrative History, 1829–1861*. New York: Macmillan, 1954.

Wilson, George. *Portrait Gallery of the Chamber of Commerce in the State of New York*. New York: Press of the Chamber of Commerce, 1890.

Wiltse, Charles M. *John C. Calhoun*. Indianapolis: Bobbs-Merrill Company, 1944.

Index